THE

MUDPIES

ACTIVITY

BOOK

RECIPES

FOR

INVENTION

By Nancy Blakey

ISBN: 0-9614626-1-2

Design and Production: Harrison Watts
Illustrations: Melissah Watts

Northwest Parent Publishing, Inc.
P.O. Box 22578
Seattle, Washington 98122

Printed in the United States of America.

TABLE OF CONTENTS

Hands On!   1-17

Crayon Soap • Bubble Solution • Float Soap • Shaving Cream Body Art • Make Your Own Superball • Sugar Cube Art • Fruit Flavored Stamps • Tap Shoes • Straw and Pipecleaner Constructs • Bone Pictures • Fast Stamp from Foot Padding • Cinnamon Dough Mobile • Styrofoam Prints • Tin Can Lantern • 3-D Salt Map Dough • Screen Pictures • Sandpaper Pictures • Geo Art Boards

Edible Art   19-31

Vegetable Vehicles • Coffee Can Gingerbread Cookies • Chocolate Pudding Fingerpaint • Chocolate Banana Pops • Ice Cream in a Coffee Can • Marzipan Art • Make Your Own Peanut Butter • Pretzels • Marshmallow Project • Doggie Donuts • Stained Glass Cookies • White Chocolate Snowmen

Celebrations   33-51

Paper Tube Party Favors • Baked Bread Birthday Crown • Party Pinata • Rubber Stamps • Standing Ghost Halloween Decoration • Robot Costume • Spooky Halloween Hands • Plaster Tape Masks • Apple Turkeys • Easy Holiday Window Decorations • Edible Holiday Cards • Christmas Ornaments • Easter Egg Extravaganza • Natural Dyes for Easter Eggs • Beeswax Candles

Science   53-75

Bean Brawn: A Weight Lifting Contest • Bottled Hurricane • Carbon Dioxide Cannon • Coloring Flowers • Dancing Raisins • Egg in a Bottle • Inside Out Balloon • Planetarium • Rubber Bones • Shining Your Pennies • Spore Soup • The Fizz Factor • Sugar Crystals • The Tooth Project • The Way Water Travels • Crack Your Marbles • Balloon Trolley • Science Shorts: Watch Me Grow —Star Dust—Sub in a Cup—The Needle and Balloon Trick

Outdoors   77-105

Beach Weaving • Dried Flowers • Fruit in a Bottle • Garden Patch • Butterfly Net • Garden Paper • Critter Cage • Beach Glass Mosaic • Weird and Wonderful Pumpkins: Personal Pumpkins— For the Biggest Pumpkin on the Block—Pumpkin with a Body • Plaster of Paris Sand Casting • To Build a Scarecrow • Spore Prints • Underwater Magnifier • Solar Prints • Nest Pickings • Let's Build Boats!: Catamaran— Power Boat—Traditional Milk Carton Boat • Message in a Bottle • Water Dredge • Super Squirts

Presents   107-119

Make Your Own Book • Bath Powder • Homemade Beads • Grapefruit Bowl • Fish Prints • Pomanders • Seed Cards • Potpourri • Sachets • Marbelized Paper

Keepsakes   121-128

Time Capsule • Seasonal Scrapbook • Photo Journal • Art Exhibit • Radio Show

HANDS-ON!

The rise of big bubbles on a spring breeze, the warm elasticity of freshly made dough, the satisfying feel of hammer to nail, are moments of discovery that celebrate the fun in creativity.

The following chapter is full of projects that encourage a loose playfulness with the materials. You can join the fun, or you can gather material for a few of these projects in a box, and take it out when you're preparing dinner, when the babysitter arrives, or when you simply need some time to yourself.

Crayon Soap

What you will need:

1 cup Ivory Snow soap
a scant 1/4 cup warm water
food coloring
muffin tin

Have your child measure the Ivory into a bowl, add the water, and stir out all the lumps. The consistency may seem a little dry, but it will eventually mix together. Add a heavy dose of food coloring until the color looks right, and spoon the mixture into the muffin tin to dry. Make additional batches for different colors. The crayons take from one to two days to dry. Pop them from the muffin tin when they are firm to the touch. Crayon soap washes off all surfaces, including the skin, with a wet washcloth.

Bubble Solution

The sheer volume of this recipe contributes to the fun of blowing bubbles!

What you will need:

12 cups cold water
1 cup liquid dish soap
2 ounces glycerine (available at your pharmacy)

Pour the water into an empty one gallon container. Add the dish soap and glycerine, and shake gently to mix.

Ideas for blowers: styrofoam cups with a pencil hole poked into the bottom; six pack rings; wire hangers bent into circles; jar lid rings; plastic berry baskets, or funnels.

Float Soap

This handmade soap is formed in cookie cutters. Insert a tiny treasure, if the soap isn't for a small child.

What you will need:

1 cup Ivory Snow soap
1/2 cup boiling water
food coloring
scented oil such as wintergreen (optional)
cookie cutters

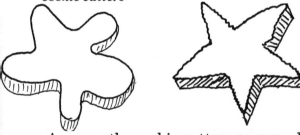

Arrange the cookie cutters on waxed paper. Measure the soap flakes into a heavy bowl and add the boiling water. Stir until the soap dissolves, and add the food coloring and scented oil if you have it. Beat the mixture with an eggbeater until it is smooth and satiny. Fill the cookie cutters and allow the soap to dry until it is firm to the touch.

Shaving Cream Body Art

Shaving cream on skin has a marvelous, velvety feel to it. Shake up a can (the foam type works best), hand it over to the artist, and watch the fun!

Make Your Own Superball

What makes a ball bounce? Find out by constructing your own superball.

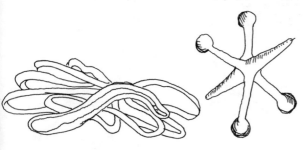

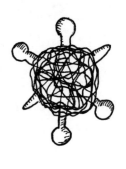

What you will need:

a metal jack (from a game of jacks)

rubber bands

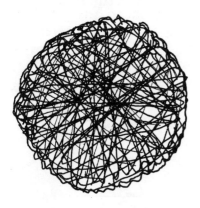

Loop, wrap, and twist the rubber bands around the jack until it is completely covered. Your child may have to experiment with the rubber bands for the best hold upon the jack. He can also cut the rubber bands and tie them together for one long rubber string to continue wrapping after the jack arms disappear. Now watch them bounce!

Sugar Cube Art

Sugar cube igloos were one of my favorite childhood projects. Our family has expanded the idea to include houses, castles, cars, battlements, or simply patterns on construction paper

What You Will Need:

sugar cubes

paste or decorator's frosting (3 egg whites, 1 lb. powdered sugar

cardboard or posterboard

If you choose to cement the cubes together with the decorator's frosting, beat the egg whites until they form peaks, then slowly add the powdered sugar. You can also add food coloring for a colorful mortar.

Fruit Flavored Stamps

What you will need:

1 tablespoon fruit-flavored gelatin

2 tablespoons hot water

pictures or words cut from the glossy pages of a magazine

Place the gelatin in a flat dish, add the hot water, and stir until dissolved. While the "stamp glue" is still warm, have the children spread it with their fingers onto the back of the pictures or words. The stamps will dry in a few hours. If they curl, flatten them in a book. When ready to use, lick the back of the stamp and apply to paper.

Tap Shoes

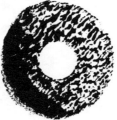

What you will need:

old pair of shoes
4-6 flat metal washers
superglue (adult use only recommended)

There was a time when nearly every pair of old shoes in our house sported taps. These are great fun. After experimenting with different types of glue, I found superglue works best and holds fast during even the most vigorous dance. Even though the actual construction of the shoes is best left to the adult, this project will provide children with hours of sheer dancing fun.

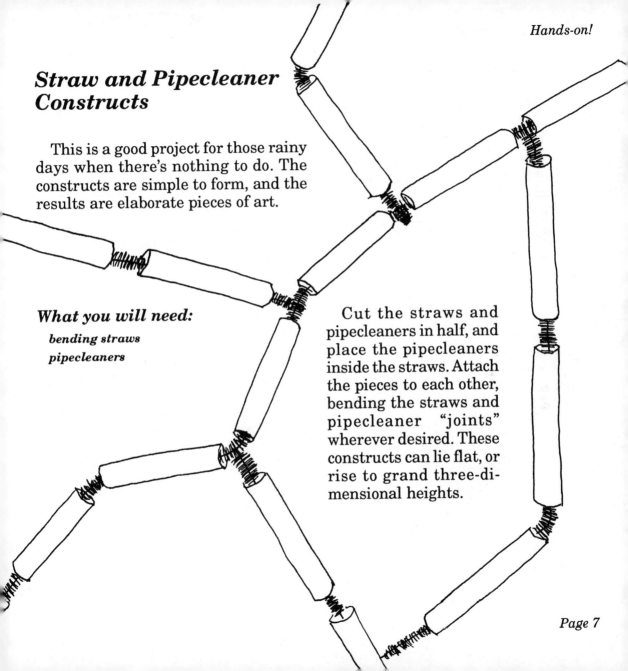

Straw and Pipecleaner Constructs

This is a good project for those rainy days when there's nothing to do. The constructs are simple to form, and the results are elaborate pieces of art.

What you will need:

bending straws
pipecleaners

Cut the straws and pipecleaners in half, and place the pipecleaners inside the straws. Attach the pieces to each other, bending the straws and pipecleaner "joints" wherever desired. These constructs can lie flat, or rise to grand three-dimensional heights.

Bone Pictures

Bleached chicken bones make dramatic pictures when they are glued onto paper or cardboard. With a little patience and forethought, your child can also glue the bones together for a creature that stands upright.

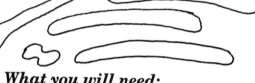

What you will need:

chicken bones

construction paper or cardboard

glue

bleach and water solution to soak the bones

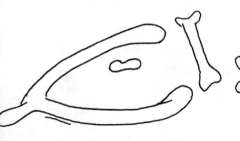

Save the chicken bones from dinner (be sure to include the back and neck if you have them), and strip them of any remaining meat. Put the bones in a pot of water and boil for half an hour. Pour a small amount of bleach in a quart jar, add water and stir. Place the boiled bones in the bleach solution for twenty four hours; then dry them thoroughly on paper towels.

When ready to use, place the bleached bones on a cookie sheet and go over the shapes with your child. Each bone has characteristics that give clues to its function: the light and delicate wing bones, the long drumstick, the flexible neck bones. Your child can then use these clues for forming her own creatures.

Fast Stamp from Foot Padding

The density of this padding makes an ideal medium for stamps. It transfers colors from felt tips beautifully, and because of the self stick backing, there is no fussing with glue. A truly fast and simple project!

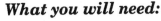

Have your child cut out a design or picture from the foot padding. Remove the paper from the adhesive side and stick the design onto the block of wood and you have a stamp! To use, rub a felt tip over the entire surface and press the stamp onto a piece of paper. These make great decorations for invitations, cards, or stationery.

What you will need:

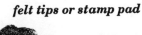

1 or 2 packages of latex foot padding (used to protect feet from shoes that rub) available at your pharmacy

small blocks of wood

scissors

felt tips or stamp pad

Cinnamon Dough Mobile

This fragrant dough has a beautiful earthy look, dries to a hard finish, and makes every breeze a spicy one.

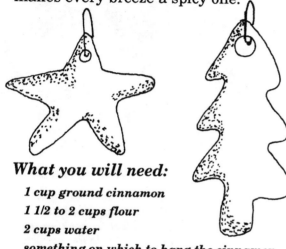

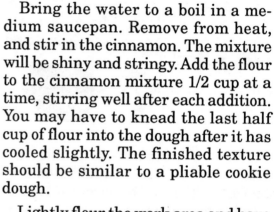

What you will need:

1 cup ground cinnamon

1 1/2 to 2 cups flour

2 cups water

something on which to hang the cinnamon cut outs (suggestions:

small basket, a piece of driftwood, an embroidery hoop)

fishing line

cookie cutters

Bring the water to a boil in a medium saucepan. Remove from heat, and stir in the cinnamon. The mixture will be shiny and stringy. Add the flour to the cinnamon mixture 1/2 cup at a time, stirring well after each addition. You may have to knead the last half cup of flour into the dough after it has cooled slightly. The finished texture should be similar to a pliable cookie dough.

Lightly flour the work area and have your child roll out the dough and cut shapes with the cookie cutters, or free form the dough into figures. Use a pencil to make a hole at the top of the shape for hanging. Dry for one or two days, then hang them from the basket or frame with the fishing line.

Styrofoam Prints

You must see this one to appreciate the first rate prints produced from nothing more than styrofoam. Although most homes will not have printer's ink and a brayer on hand, they are valuable tools to learn to work with and are remarkably inexpensive. (Note: water-based ink wipes up easily and can be used for fish prints as well.)

What you will need:
  styrofoam trays
  water-based printer's ink
  brayer

Have your child cut the styrofoam tray into a few large pieces. Scratch a picture onto a styrofoam piece with a blunt pencil to make a clear imprint, but do not pierce the styrofoam completely.

Squirt some ink onto a flat dish or tray and roll the brayer back and forth across the ink to spread it evenly over the roller. Roll the inked brayer completely over the picture and press the print gently but firmly onto a piece of paper. Isn't it beautiful?

Tin Can Lantern

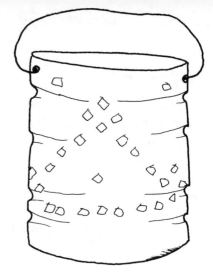

This project is one of my family's all-time favorites. Used extensively in Colonial America, these lanterns provide a relatively safe way for your child to carry a candle (under adult supervision of course!). Perhaps part of this project's appeal lies not only in the process of creating something unique, but also in the child's role as giver of light.

What you will need:

tin cans: any size, but big ones are best. Boston brown bread comes in a coated can that reflects light beautifully (available at your grocer in the bean section).

candles: no higher than 1" below the top of the can

hammer and nail

coat hanger or wire to be used for a handle

dried spaghetti noodle (for lighting the candles)

towel for each can

Fill each clean and empty can with water and freeze solid. The ice will keep the can from collapsing when holes are nailed into the sides.

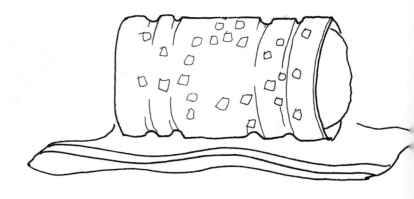

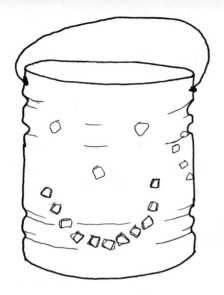

When the cans are ready, provide each lantern maker with a hammer and a good sized nail. Lay the can of ice on a folded towel to prevent it from slipping, and have your child nail holes into the sides of the lantern. The more holes, the more light the lantern will emit when it is lit. Your child can nail random holes, or follow a pattern drawn on the side with a felt tip before the can is frozen.

To make a handle, nail two holes near the top of the can on opposite sides. Slip the wire hanger through the holes, and bend the ends to hold it in place. To light the lantern, drip a little wax on the bottom of the can for securing the candle firmly into place. Lighting the candles in the lantern is much easier with a dried spaghetti noodle. The long piece of pasta burns steadily and allows time to light each candle without burning fingers.

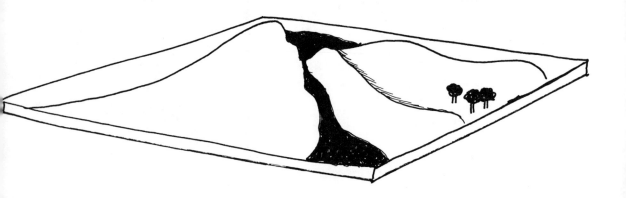

3-D Salt Map Dough

This dough is a versatile art medium for many projects. We have made three-dimensional party invitations, maps of imaginary lands, and raised pictures that, when painted, give a wonderfully different aspect to drawn art.

What you will need:

3 cups white flour

3 cups salt

2 cups water (approximately)

cardboard, or posterboard, foam core board, or thin plywood

poster paints

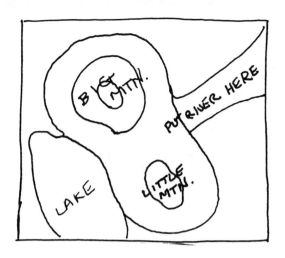

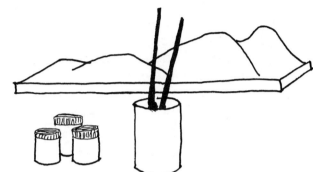

Mix the salt and flour together, and add enough water so the dough is the consistency of frosting. The more water you use, the longer it will take to dry.

Have your child draw a map or picture on the posterboard. The map can be a familiar place or an imaginary place with volcanoes, lakes, rivers and mountains. Spread the mixture within the drawn boundaries, piling it to form the mountains, and scraping through the dough with a pencil or finger to form the river beds and lakes.

After it is dry, (anywhere from 1 to 3 days depending upon the thickness of dough and humidity in the air), paint with poster paints.

Screen Pictures

Placing screen under drawing paper gives a new look to crayoned pictures because of the screen's interesting graph-like pattern. It provides a unique texture and added dimension to ordinary crayoned art.

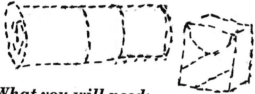

What you will need:

screen (available in small rolls at your hardware store)

crayons

paper

Cut the screen slightly larger than the sheet of paper your child will be using. Place the paper over the screen and color as usual. The screen creates a novel texture on the picture, almost as if it were done on a "coloring computer" as one child described These pictures make wonderful cards when they are cut and matted on flexible cardboard.

Geo-Art Boards

Sandpaper Pictures

Crayons work differently on sandpaper, producing dense colors not possible on regular paper.

What you will need:

fine sandpaper

crayons

Have your child draw a picture on the sandpaper. Place the drawing on a cookie sheet and put it in a 225 degree oven for 30 seconds. The wax will melt into a paint-like finish. The picture can also be left as is for the deep-colored effect.

What you will need:

block of wood

nails

rubber bands (all sizes and shapes)

strings of different colors

hammer

Have your child hammer the nails halfway into the wood in any pattern desired. Then loop the rubber bands and string around the nails to create designs and unusual shapes. A geo-art board can also become a musical instrument or a marble maze.

EDIBLE ART

Take a bowlful of chocolate pudding, a few pieces of paper, and a group of children, and you have a recipe for fun! Not all of the projects in this chapter are as delightfully messy as pudding fingerpaint, but transforming food into art, whether in the form of pretzels or three dimensional marshmallow structures, can make an ordinary day a festive occasion. Try coffee can ice cream on the first day of summer, or marzipan art on a lazy afternoon.

Vegetable Vehicles

Provide any or all of the following ingredients and have your child use the toothpicks to assemble cars, airplanes, etc. The fun of working creatively with these familiar ingredients might encourage finicky appetites. Be sure to watch for hidden toothpicks when eating the creations.

What you will need:

toothpicks and:
carrot rounds
celery
cherry tomatoes
cubed potatoes and turnips
zucchinis
red cabbage strips
green beans
fresh peas
mushrooms
broccoli stems
radishes
sweet peppers

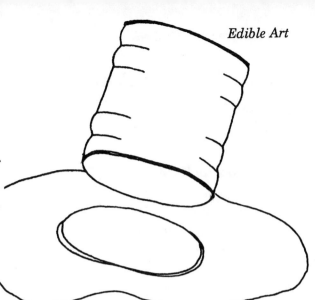

Coffee Can Gingerbread Cookies

Huge cookies with an expanse to decorate! These beauties make great gifts. Lay them individually on a bed of Easter grass in a shallow box. Make a cover with plastic wrap, and add a ribbon.

What you will need:

1 cup butter or margarine

1 cup sugar

1 cup dark molasses

1/3 cup water

4 cups flour

1 teaspoon baking soda

2 teaspoons ginger

1/2 teaspoon nutmeg

2 teaspoons cinnamon candies, currants, raisins for decorating

Cream the butter and sugar. Mix in the remaining ingredients. Cover and chill for two hours. Roll out the dough on a lightly-floured surface. Cut the cookies with a 1 pound coffee can with both ends removed (file down any sharp edges around the rims). Decorate and bake at 375 degrees for 10 to 12 minutes.

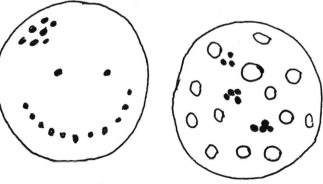

Chocolate Pudding Fingerpaint

What you will need:

1 package instant choco-late pudding

shelf paper (for printing)

cookie sheet or tray

Have your child make the pudding according to directions, and pour it onto the tray or cookie sheet. Fingerpaint directly on the tray. To make a print of the painting, gently lay a piece of shelf paper on top of the pudding design, and press very lightly over the entire surface. Pull the pudding print up carefully, and allow to dry.

Chocolate Banana Pops

What you will need:

4 peeled bananas

1 cup chocolate chips

2 tablespoons water

popsicle sticks

coconut or chopped nuts

Melt the chocolate chips in a double boiler or in the microwave. Stir in the water. Have your child push a popsicle stick into each banana, and roll it in the melted chocolate until it is well coated. Sprinkle the coconut or chopped nuts over the chocolate. Place the pops on a plate and freeze until hard.

Ice Cream in a Coffee Can

You don't need an ice cream maker for this one, and your child is involved at every stage.

Have your child stir the milk, whipping cream, sugar, vanilla, and fruit or nuts together in the small coffee can. Put the plastic lid on, and place the can inside the larger coffee can. Pack the ice into the large can around the small can, and sprinkle 1 cup rock salt over it. Put the plastic lid securely on the large can, and start rolling!

Roll the can across the floor for approximately 10 minutes, then stir the ice cream mixture from the sides. Drain the large can and add more ice and salt if necessary. Roll until the ice cream has hardened. Enjoy it from the can.

What you will need:

1 cup milk

1 cup whipping cream

1/2 cup sugar

1/2 teaspoon vanilla

fruits or nuts

ice

rock salt

large (2 lb. 7 oz.) coffee can with plastic lid

small (1 lb.) coffee can with plastic lid

Marzipan Art

Marzipan, an almond paste confection, comes in prepared tubes at your grocery store. The texture is a wonderful cross between playdough and modelling clay, and it holds it shape even after vigorous handling, allowing your child to create ingenious decorations for cakes and cookies.

Take a small piece of the marzipan and work in drops of food coloring until the desired color is reached. When making the decorations, work with small portions. Marzipan is rich, and there is something special about a tiny version of ducks or a bunch of grapes. Marzipan art pieces can be used immediately, or left to dry.

Make Your Own Peanut Butter

What you will need:

peanuts
vegetable oil

If you are using peanuts in the shell, rub the skin off the nuts, and save the shells for making finger puppets. Place the nuts in a blender and grind them to a paste, adding oil a little at a time until the peanut butter is the desired consistency. Add salt to taste, and enjoy! Refrigerate the leftover peanut butter in a covered jar.

Pretzels

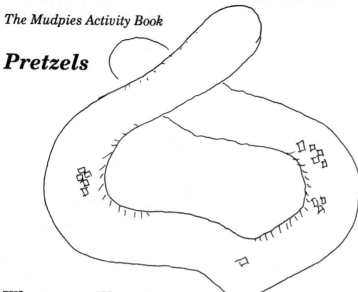

What you will need:

1 cup water

2 tablespoons sugar

2 pkgs. dry yeast (fast acting yeast will have the dough ready in half the time)

1 egg

3 1/2 to 4 cups flour (approximately)

coarse salt (kosher)

Have your child stir the yeast, sugar, and warm water together in a large bowl until the yeast is dissolved. Set aside to "proof," or get foamy (about 15-20 minutes). While you are waiting, explain that the yeast is actually tiny plants that grow by using the sugar/water mixture for food.

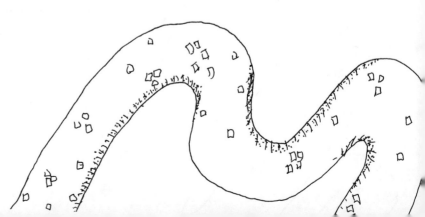

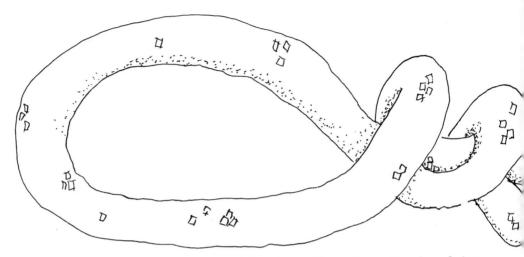

After the yeast proofs, stir in the flour a little at a time, until the dough is stiff. Knead on a floured surface for three to five minutes. If you or your child have never kneaded dough before, think of it as a punching, rolling game. Don't worry about doing it the "right" way; the dough will still rise and taste delicious.

After kneading, form the dough into a ball, and place it in a buttered bowl. Cover with a dish towel, and let it rise in a warm place until doubled in size (about an hour unless you are using fast acting yeast). After the dough has risen, punch it down (the fun part!), roll it into a rectangle, and cut fat strips to shape into pretzels. Any shape your child comes up with is a pretzel!

Beat the egg with a fork and brush onto the pretzels. Sprinkle on salt to taste. Bake in a 400 degree oven 10-15 minutes, or until golden brown.

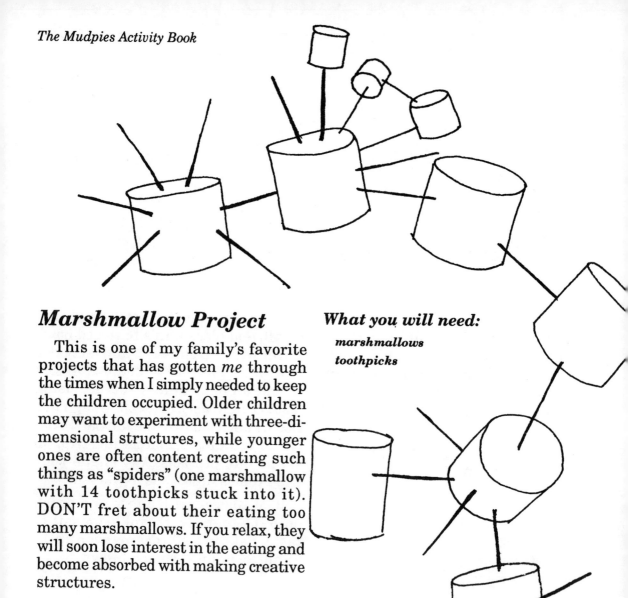

Marshmallow Project

This is one of my family's favorite projects that has gotten *me* through the times when I simply needed to keep the children occupied. Older children may want to experiment with three-dimensional structures, while younger ones are often content creating such things as "spiders" (one marshmallow with 14 toothpicks stuck into it). DON'T fret about their eating too many marshmallows. If you relax, they will soon lose interest in the eating and become absorbed with making creative structures.

What you will need:

marshmallows
toothpicks

Doggie Donuts

This treat for your favorite dog is a unique example of creating a common grocery store product from scratch.

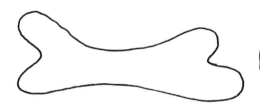

What you will need:

2 cups wheat germ

1 cup cornmeal

1 cup rye flour (you can substitute wheat or white flour)

2 cups whole wheat flour

3 1/2 - 4 cups white flour

4 teaspoons salt

1 egg

1 package yeast

2 cups warm water

1 can condensed chicken broth

Have your child mix the dry ingredients in a large bowl with her hands. Add the egg, chicken broth, and warm water and stir with a wooden spoon until a lump of dough forms. You may have to take over at this point; the dough gets pretty stiff. Add more flour if necessary so the dough is not too sticky for little hands. Flour the work area and roll donuts or cut bones from the dough. Bake on a greased cookie sheet at 300 degrees for 45 minutes.

Stained Glass Cookies

Each cookie is a feast for the eyes!

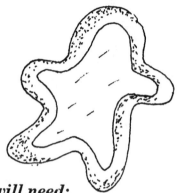

What you will need:

1 cup sugar

4 tablespoons butter

1 egg

3 tablespoons milk

1 teaspoon vanilla

2 1/4 cups flour

1 teaspoon baking powder

crushed hard candy pieces
(suckers work well)

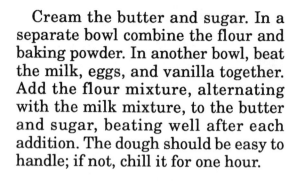

Cream the butter and sugar. In a separate bowl combine the flour and baking powder. In another bowl, beat the milk, eggs, and vanilla together. Add the flour mixture, alternating with the milk mixture, to the butter and sugar, beating well after each addition. The dough should be easy to handle; if not, chill it for one hour.

Give your child some dough and have her roll it into skinny snakes. Bend each snake into a design on a foil covered cookie sheet, and pinch the ends together. Sprinkle a thin layer of the crushed candy into the enclosed space. You can make wheels, snowmen, butterflies, the sun, even eyeglasses. Just be sure the ends are sealed so the melted candy won't leak out. Bake at 375 degrees for 9 minutes. Allow to cool, and peel off the foil.

White Chocolate Snowmen

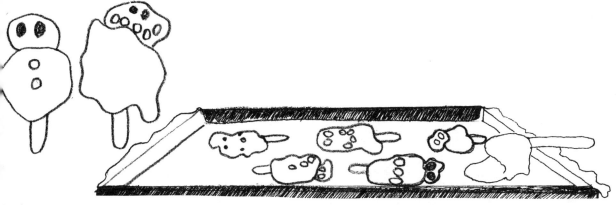

What you will need:

1 lb. white chocolate

raisins

cinnamon candies

straws or popsicle sticks

wax paper

Break the chocolate into pieces and melt in a double boiler or in the microwave, following manufacturer's directions.

Line a cookie sheet with buttered wax paper, and have your child spoon the melted chocolate onto the wax paper. Don't worry if the design looks more like a protozoa - it will still taste delicious! To decorate, press the candies and raisins into the chocolate before it hardens, and place the straw or popsicle stick into the snowman for a handle. To anchor the handle more securely, cover it with more chocolate.

CELEBRATIONS

Birthdays, Halloween, and the seasonal holidays are magical times for children. They count the days to a party, plan costumes in July, and pace the year off by holiday ("What comes after Valentine's Day?") Celebrate with projects that make special occasions a process!

Paper Tube Party Favors

Once your children do this project, you will never be allowed to throw out toilet paper tubes again. Mine are fished from the garbage to be used at every party we give.

What you will need:

toilet paper tubes

felt tips

construction paper

clear wide package tape

different types of candies

tiny treasures: erasers, marbles, jacks, rings, etc.

Optional: bingo markers (bright nontoxic markers with a sponge applicator available wherever bingo is played)

Give each child a paper tube to decorate with the felt tips and bingo markers. When they are finished, tape one end with the packaging tape, leaving the other end open. Have the children fill the tubes with the candies and treasures and then seal the open end with the tape.

After the tubes are sealed, have the children use the construction paper to make witches' brooms, rockets, Christmas trees, flowers, pencils, telescopes, etc., depending upon the occasion.

Baked Bread Birthday Crown

What you will need:

2 loaves frozen dough

1 egg, beaten

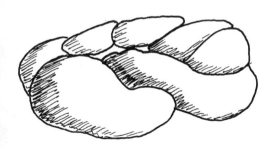

Place the dough in a big buttered pan, cover with a lid, and let rise to double in size. Have your child punch the loaves down; then make a long skinny rope out of each loaf. Twist the two ropes loosely together, and make a ring or crown out of the twisted dough on a greased cookie sheet. Seal the edges, and brush the beaten egg on the crown for a shiny, golden effect. Let rise to double in size, about 30 to 60 minutes, and bake at 375 degrees for 25 to 30 minutes.

Party Piñata

What you will need:

For the paste:
1-3/4 cups water
1/4 cup sugar
1/4 cup flour
1/2 teaspoon alum

For the piñata:
1 large balloon
strips of newspaper 2"
wide
sponge-tipped paintbrush
(1" wide)
poster paint
string for hanging the
piñata
candy and prizes

Mix together the flour, sugar, and alum. Slowly add one cup of the water, stirring to work out all the lumps. Boil the mixture, stirring constantly, until the paste is smooth and clear. Add the remainder of the water, and mix well. Allow the paste to cool before using on the inflated balloon.

Blow up the balloon and tie. If the paste is too thick, add a little water for easier spreading. Lay the strips out on newspaper and have your child brush the paste on them with the sponge-tipped paintbrush. You can also dip the strips directly into the paste, but the drying time will be longer.

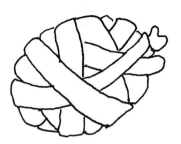

Cover the balloon with crisscrossed layers of paste-covered newspaper strips. If you have younger children eager to help, provide a smaller balloon for them to wrap strips on any way they like.

The number of layers to lay on the balloon will depend on the ages of the children at the party. You want everyone to have a turn hitting the piñata, but you don't want it too difficult to burst. For small children, two to three layers is sufficient. For older children and adults, add up to four layers. Leave a space at the top of the balloon for an opening, and cover it later with construction paper or a hat.

Allow one to two days for drying, and then pop the balloon. Be careful; if the papier mache is still damp, the piñata will cave in with the collapse of the balloon.

After the balloon is popped, have your child paint the piñata. To hang it after the paint dries, poke three to four holes about three inches down from the opening and reinforce the holes with tape and tie on the strings to the length desired.

For the party, ask your guests to bring a contribution for the piñata, and add the prizes as they arrive. Consider other things besides candy: whistles, erasers, small rubber balls, and popcorn are a few ideas.

Preschoolers may find hitting the piñata challenging enough without being blindfolded. Hand over the plastic bat, stand back and watch the fun!

Rubber Stamps

Use these unique handmade stamps to decorate poster paper for a special gift wrap. They are also fun to use when making birthday or holiday cards.

What you will need:

pieces of rubber inner tube (the leaky ones are often free at tire stores)

a small block of wood

stamp pad or felt tip pens

rubber cement

pocketknife

Cut a piece of inner tube to fit the piece of wood. Ask your child to draw something simple on the piece of inner tube, then carefully cut the drawing out. Brush rubber cement on the inside of the inner tube (the smooth rubber side must face out), and on the block of wood. Wait a few seconds, then press them firmly together. An adult should cut and assemble the stamp for younger children. After the glue sets, the stamp is ready to use with felt tip pens or a stamp pad.

These stamps make a nice gift for children ages two and up when they're accompanied by a set of felt tips or a stamp pad. A child's name or a holiday symbol can be carved on the stamp to mark a special occasion.

Standing Ghost Halloween Decoration

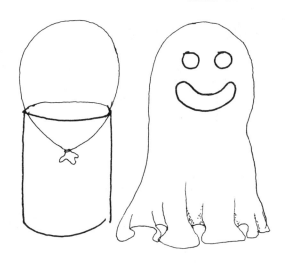

Blow up the balloon, tie, and place it on top of the canning jar; or place a styrofoam ball onto a large soda bottle (stick a pencil into the ball and lower it into the bottle to keep it secure).

Cut the cheesecloth into long enough sections to cover the form, and drape onto the table for a ghostly look. Cover the table area with newspapers to catch the drips from the starch, and have your child pour the liquid starch into a large bowl.

Dip the cheesecloth pieces into the starch, wring out the excess, and drape over the balloon and bottle. Lay several layers over the bottle and allow to dry completely. Pull out the bottle and balloon, and the ghost will stand on its own! Finish decorating the ghost with black construction paper cut outs for the mouth and eyes.

What you will need:

cheesecloth

liquid starch

tall bottle: quart canning jar or soda bottle

small balloon, or styrofoam ball

black construction paper

Robot Costume

This costume comes with no directions. The following items are suggestions for children to use in creating their own version of a robot. You will be amazed at the delightful details they will come up with that may never occur to an adult!

An adult may have to help match the box size to the child's size in order to make sure the child doesn't create a masterpiece costume that is too small or too large. Spray paint the boxes gold or silver the day before the project begins. A hot glue gun is a worthwhile investment to bond the materials to the boxes quickly and efficiently.

Then step back and watch an artist at work!

What You Can Use:

boxes (all sizes for head and body)

dryer vent hose (for arms and legs)

buttons

wire

pipe cleaners

Styrofoam cups and plates

poster paints

foil

fluorescent tape

electrical tape

wide packing tape

mylar

toilet paper and paper towel tubes

air bubble packing wrap

Styrofoam packing material

old jewelry

nuts and bolts

felt tip pens

stapler

glue (hot glue gun optional)

knife, scissors, utility knife (with adult supervision)

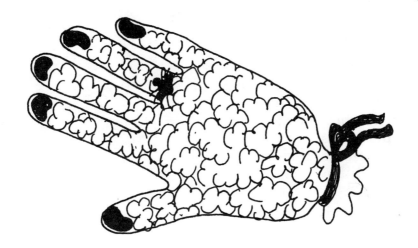

Spooky Halloween Hands

What you will need:

*clear disposable gloves
(food handler gloves work
well)*

jelly beans

popcorn

plastic spider ring

ribbon

Have the children stuff a jelly bean into each finger of the glove for a fingernail. Or they can stuff the fingers entirely with jelly beans! Fill the rest of the glove with popcorn, and fasten the open end with the ribbon. For the final touch, slip a spider ring onto a finger.

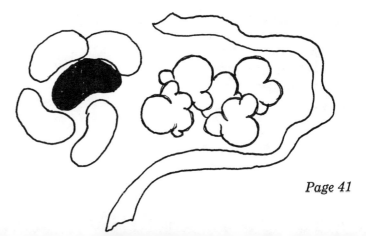

Plaster Tape Masks

Making plaster masks is a gentle process that encourages paying close attention to your partner's feelings. Small children may not like the feel or look of plaster on faces, but I highly recommend this project for older children and adults.

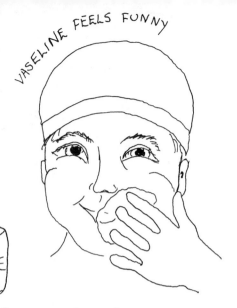

What you will need:

plaster tape (available at art supply, or medical supply outlets)

Vaseline

newspapers

bowl of warm water

towel

decorating materials: paints, glitter, sequins, feathers, etc.

shower cap

1/2 inch elastic

Before starting, the mask person needs to tuck all his hair into the shower cap, and spread Vaseline liberally over his face, including his eyebrows and hairline, to prevent the plaster from sticking as it dries.

Meanwhile, the person making the mask can cut the plaster tape into various lengths ranging from three to six inches. Lay newspapers over the work area, and bring the bowl of warm water, and strips of tape within easy reach. Have the mask person lie down on the newspapers, instead of sitting in a chair. It makes the process more relaxing and less messy.

THE PLASTER TAPE LOOKS SCARY

BACK TO NORMAL

You are now ready to make the mask. Use one of the longer plaster strips, and dip it into the bowl of warm water. Squeeze out the excess water, and lay it along the outer edges of the face. Continue laying the strips, smoothing the plaster strips with your fingers as you go. Work your way inwards, saving the shorter pieces of tape for detailing the nose, lips and around the eyes. Leave a space for breathing below the nose, and leave the eyes clear. Lay at least two layers of plaster strips.

When the plaster tingles, it has begun to set. You can safely remove the mask when it lifts from the face in one piece. Allow it to dry thoroughly, and punch holes with a paper punch or a corkscrew for the elastic to be strung through.

Your child can build up features on the mask with modelling paste, and paint it after it has dried overnight.

Apple Turkeys

I remember this project from my childhood in Idaho. Apple turkeys have never lost their appeal to children, and after making these, various forms of the bird will appear year round in your home.

What you will need:

apples
toothpicks
marshmallows
raisins
raw carrot rounds
fresh cranberries
gumdrops

The construction of an apple turkey can be as elaborate or simple as the creator wishes. Older children may want to fashion something that resembles a turkey, while the younger ones, uninhibited by form, can produce wonderful creatures that are turkeys in name only. Provide the materials without instruction, and see what your child's imagination produces.

Easy Holiday Window Decorations

This project for all ages requires only a bottle of white shoe polish with a sponge applicator, a window, and a child's imagination. Have your child paint snowmen and snowflakes for Christmas, or ghosts for Halloween, directly onto a window.

The beauty of white shoe polish is that it's clean, does not drip easily, and wipes off with a wet rag when the holidays are over.

Edible Holiday Cards

This gingerbread dough holds up well during the holiday season whether you decide to hang the cards on your tree or send them through the mail (protected, of course, with a cardboard "sandwich".)

What you will need:

2 cups molasses
1 cup oil
6-1/2 cups flour
1 teaspoon ginger
1 teaspoon soda
1 teaspoon salt

Decorator's Frosting:
3 egg whites
1 lb. powdered sugar
pinch cream of tartar
candies, currants, raisins, sprinkles

To make the dough, stir the molasses and oil together. Add the flour, ginger, soda, and salt and mix well.

Flour the work area, and have your child roll out the dough. Then cut squares and rectangles, or use large cookie cutters to form the "cards." Make a hole near the top with an un-sharpened pencil for stringing the ribbon through, and decorate the cookies with the candies, currants and raisins. Bake 10 minutes on a greased cookie sheet.

Make decorator's frosting by beating the egg whites until stiff, then stir in the powdered sugar and cream of tartar. If you don't have a cake decorating bag, place the frosting in a small plastic bag with a tiny bit cut from a corner and have your child squeeze. When the frosting has hardened, string a ribbon through the hole and hang the card on the tree, or place it in a decorated envelope.

Christmas Ornaments

Don't let plaster of paris intimidate you. It is cheap, easy to use, and surprisingly neat, if purchased in a squeeze bottle.

What you will need:

plaster of paris

plastic candy molds (available at variety stores)

squeeze bottles: the kind for mustard and ketchup

ornament hooks

poster paints

Mix the plaster of paris according to the directions. Mix it in a bowl that has a lip for pouring, or use a funnel to fill the squeeze bottles. Provide a variety of molds, and have the children fill them with the plaster of paris. Press an ornament hook into the plaster while it is still wet. Allow the ornaments to dry completely (approximately eight hours) before applying the poster paints.

Easter Egg Extravaganza

The whole family will want to get in on the action. Be sure to have plenty of eggs on hand!

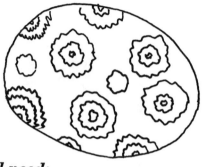

What you will need:

For striped eggs:
narrow masking tape
wide rubber bands
prepared egg dyes
hard-cooked eggs

For leaf imprinted eggs:
onion skin dye (Boil 4 cups water and 2 cups onion skins for 20 minutes)
lacy leaves or ferns
pieces of nylon stocking
rubber bands
raw eggs

For batik eggs:
hard-cooked eggs
candle
prepared egg dyes
1 tablespoon baking soda dissolved in 1 cup water

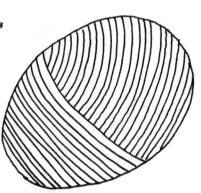

For striped eggs, dye the eggs in the prepared dye. Place the rubber bands securely around the eggs and dye again in a different color. For plaid eggs, use the same method, only use the narrow masking tape to tape lengthwise stripes. For a checkered effect, dye again after the tape has been placed.

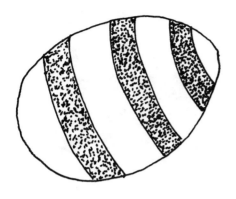

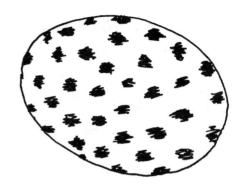

For the leaf imprint eggs, slip a raw egg into a piece of nylon stocking. Carefully place the leaves around the egg, and secure the ends of the nylon with rubber bands to hold the leaves in place. Boil in the onion skin solution for fifteen minutes. Cool and unwrap.

For the batik eggs, dribble wax from a burning candle onto the egg before coloring. Dye in the prepared solution, and rub off the wax after warming the egg in a slightly warm oven. For reverse batik, dye the eggs then dribble the wax onto the shell. Bleach the color off the egg in the soda/water solution. (It may take up to ten minutes.) Dye again, or leave the egg white with its dark drips of color.

Natural Dyes for Easter Eggs

Beautiful earthy hues help to celebrate the turning of seasons and the rebirth of spring. These eggs make a splendid centerpiece when they're displayed in a rustic basket of fresh leaves.

What you will need:

2-1/2 cups water

2 tablespoons vinegar

For magenta:
2 cups chopped beetroot

For blue:
2 cups blueberries

For burnt sienna:
2 cups yellow onion skins
4 cups water

Have your child combine the measured coloring agent with the water in a pan. Bring to a boil, cover, and simmer for twenty minutes. Strain the dye through a colander into another pan. Cool and stir in the vinegar; then pour into a glass or jar suitable for dying eggs. Be careful — these dyes can stain clothing.

Experiment with different ideas for dyes. Ask your child what she thinks would dye an egg: mustard? blackberries? grass? Then try it!

Beeswax Candles

These candles are flawlessly simple, allowing plenty of room for self expression. The ingredients are found at candle making supply or hobby shops, and are worth the trouble of finding!

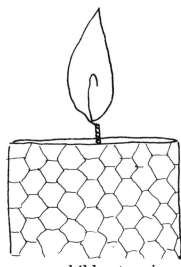

What you will need:

beeswax: comes in 8"x16" sheets in a wide variety of colors

wick

glitter or sequins (optional)

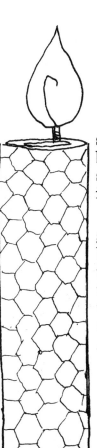

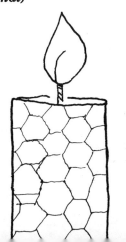

Have your child cut a piece of wick slightly longer than the width of the beeswax and press it firmly into the sheet close to the edge. Roll the wax into a cylinder and there's your candle!

Experiment! Scatter the sequins or glitter on a piece of paper and lay the beeswax on top before rolling. Roll on the bias, or press a number of sheets together for a big candle. Cut the beeswax into different sizes for birthday candles, jack-o-lantern lights, and Advent or Hanukkah candles.

SCIENCE

Sunday nights are experiment nights in our household. Somehow I missed science in my own formal education, perhaps because it seemed inaccessible with its dry facts-and-formula overtones, and later I felt a whole world of exciting information had passed me by.

The experiments in this chapter are fun. There are cannons that pop, solutions that fume and fizz, and marbles that crack. Even if children see the results as nothing more than magic, their worlds will enlarge with a science that invites speculation and welcomes the big question, "Why?"

Bean Brawn: A Weight Lifting Contest

The force of a sprouting seed can crack rocks and split cement. With this project a child can explore a seed's power, and marvel at its tenacity for survival.

What you will need:

10 dried beans: any kind will do

toothpicks

pennies

tray or dish suitable to plant in

potting soil

Have your child soak the beans in water overnight for faster germination. Pour the potting soil into a big bowl and stir in enough water to dampen. Pat the soil into the tray and push a soaked bean in about a half inch. Cover lightly with soil and place a penny on top.

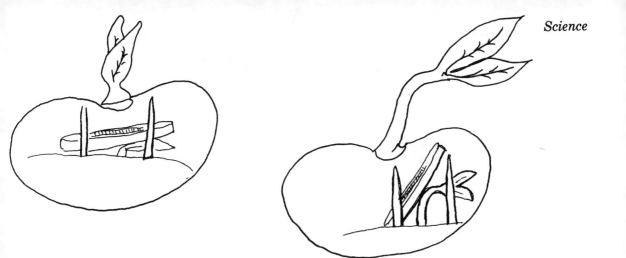

Make a "fence" around the penny with the toothpicks to prevent it from toppling off to the side as the seed sprouts. Push another bean into the soil and add two pennies. The next bean add three, and so on until the tenth bean has ten pennies inside its fence! Keep the soil damp until germination takes place.

The results may surprise you. Each bean has its own genes for "muscle," and sometimes the sprout with three pennies, for example, will heft its weight more quickly than one with less.

Bottled Hurricane

Capture the exciting form of a hurricane in a soda bottle! Adults may need to help with the assembly, but the thrill of creating a cyclonic storm is left to your child.

What you will need:

2 soda bottles, large or small works fine

steel washer with a small hole, the same width as the bottle openings

electrical tape

Fill one of the bottles three fourths full of water. Tape the washer to the opening by crisscrossing the tape over the washer and bottle, and then cutting the hole open again with a small knife. Place the other bottle upside down on top of the taped washer, and tape securely into place.

To make the hurricane, have your child flip the bottles over, water on top, and place them on a table. Quickly grasp the lower bottle with one hand and the upper bottle with the other. Move the top bottle in a wide circle before the water runs down, and watch the whirling formation of a hurricane between your fingers!

Carbon Dioxide Cannon

There are science experiments you do one time, and science experiments that children ask for over and over. This cannon belongs to the latter category! It pops dramatically, and is simple to make with a few ingredients found in your home.

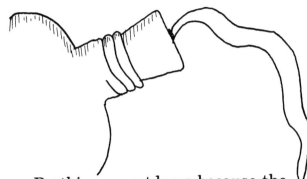

What you will need:

vinegar

water

baking soda

bottle with a cork: a large soda bottle, and a cork from the hardware store works well

crepe paper

Do this one outdoors because the cork really flies! To keep track of its path, pin or glue crepe paper streamers to the cork. Pour a little water into the bottle and add a half cup of vinegar. Crease a small piece of paper and put a heaping spoon of baking soda onto it. Slide the soda into the bottle, and quickly place the cork.(It helps if you wet the cork before putting it into the bottle.)

Be sure the cannon is not pointing at anybody, as the cork is thrust out of the bottle with the same force that, on a grander scale, launches rockets into outer space.

Coloring Flowers

Demonstrate how water circulates in plants with this variation on the celery-in-red-water theme.

What you will need:

*light colored flowers:
narcissus, daffodils,
daisies, Queen Anne Lace,
carnations, etc.*

food coloring

water

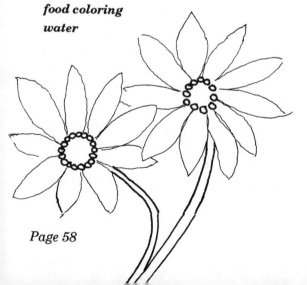

Fill a large jar with water, and stir in several drops of food coloring. Cut the flower stems at an angle for better water absorption, and place the flowers in the jar. Talk to your child about how water continually rises from the roots of a plant to the leaves, keeping it nourished and growing.

It takes a few days for the flower heads to change color, but the wait is worth it!

Dancing Raisins

The proportions of ingredients are flexible, making this project easy enough for young children to do entirely by themselves.

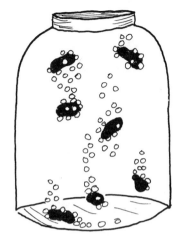

What you will need:

glass jar (pint size)
water
raisins
vinegar
soda

Fill the jar with water and add several tablespoons of vinegar. Stir it up and add a few raisins. Add a tablespoon of soda without stirring and watch the dance begin!

Bubbles of carbon dioxide form by mixing the soda (a base), with the vinegar (an acid). These small bubbles attach to the skin of the raisins, causing them to rise to the surface, and then as the bubbles pop, to sink down again. It is a wonder to watch, and the effect can last for over an hour.

Egg in a Bottle

Experiments that go "pop" are like magnets to children. This experiment explores the concepts of gases taking up space, and air pressure.

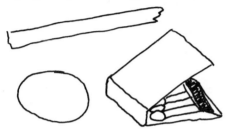

What you will need:

old fashioned milk bottle, or 8 oz. glass baby bottle

eggs: medium to small

vinegar

matches and small piece of paper

oil

Soak a few eggs in vinegar overnight. This is a fun experiment in itself. The vinegar leaches out the calcium from the egg shell and leaves it flexible and rubbery (see "Rubber Bones."). Hard boil a few more eggs, and peel.

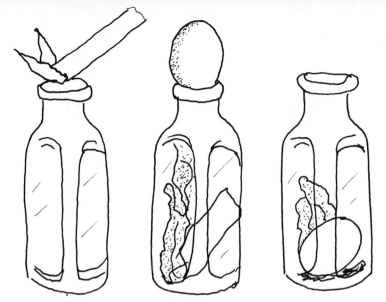

To make it easier for the eggs to slip in, oil the egg and the mouth of the bottle. Light the small piece of paper and drop it into the bottle. Quickly place the vinegared egg upon the mouth of the bottle. The burning paper will extinguish, and the egg is drawn into the bottle with a dramatic "pop!" Try it with your other eggs.

Gases inside the bottle are heated by the flame and expand. When the fire goes out, the gases contract again. The egg acts as a seal and is drawn into the bottle because of the lowered air pressure. There is more space in the bottle when the gases contract, and the egg has no choice but to fill it. Even if the egg breaks during its descent, this experiment still explores the concepts of expansion, contraction and air pressure.

Inside Out Balloon

How is it possible for a balloon to be drawn into a bottle, and inflate full size before our eyes?

What you will need:

steel wool pad without soap

vinegar

balloon

narrow necked bottle (a large soda bottle works well)

pencil

6 drops of water

Soak the steel wool pad in vinegar for a few minutes. The vinegar removes the protective coating and permits the iron in the steel wool to rust quickly.

Remove the pad, and shake the excess vinegar off. Pull the steel wool into threads and poke them into the bottle with a pencil. Add six drops of water, and place the balloon over the opening.

The rusting process uses the oxygen in the bottle. This leaves space inside, lowers the air pressure, and allows the heavier outside air to push the balloon into the bottle and inflates it. You have to see it to believe it!

Planetarium

The bedroom ceiling becomes a night sky of stars with this easy to make planetarium.

What you will need:
cereal box
pencil
flashlight

Have your child poke holes into the bottom of the cereal box with a pencil. Suggest the shape of one of the major constellations such as the Big Dipper, or let him create the Milky Way!

In the dark before bedtime, shine the flashlight into the cereal box and observe the "stars" your child created.

This is a good introduction to the constellations and their legends. Check out a book from the children's section in the library, and read it together to share an uncomplicated introduction to the stars.

Rubber Bones

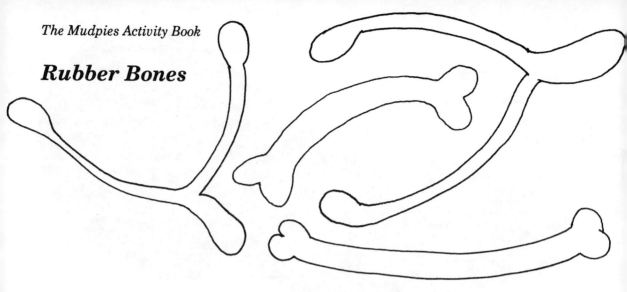

What you will need:

vinegar

chicken bones: include a wishbone: they "rubberize" faster

two glasses

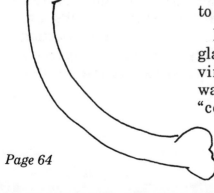

Have your child clean the bones and examine them closely. Do they flex? Can they break? Explain that calcium is what makes our bones hard and firm, and without it, our bones would be like rubber bands, unable to hold our bodies up.

Place a bone in each glass and cover one with vinegar, and one with water. The water is your "control" to judge the bones by. Replace the water and vinegar twice a week.

In two or three weeks, the bones in the vinegar will be flexible because the vinegar, an acid, changed the calcium phosphate in the bones into calcium acetate. Calcium acetate is water soluble and leaches out of the bones, leaving them like rubber.

Shining Your Pennies

Is there fun in "chemical reactions?" Find out with this simple experiment.

What you will need:

vinegar
salt
three glasses
water

Place the three glasses before your child, and have her put approximately one inch of vinegar in two glasses, and one inch of salt in the other. Add one teaspoon salt to a glass with the vinegar, and a little water to the glass with the salt.

You now have three solutions: one with both salt and vinegar, one with salt and water, and one with vinegar only. Talk about the ingredients of each glass with your child and label them. Add tarnished pennies to all three glasses and wait fifteen to twenty minutes for the results.

Only the pennies in the salt and vinegar solution are shiny because of a chemical reaction that occurs when salt and vinegar mix. The other solutions could not do the trick because they needed a "helper" chemical.

Spore Soup

Molds are a type of plant grown from spores, tiny seeds found nearly everywhere. When cultivated on a dark surface, like tomato soup, their weird beauty is visible to the naked eye.

What you will need:

tomato soup
dirt from under fingernails
bread crumbs
floor dirt
plastic wrap
magnifying glass

Pour a little prepared tomato soup into three flat dishes. Scrape the fingernail dirt onto the surface of one dish, a pinch of floor dirt onto another, and a few bread crumbs onto the last dish. Cover with the plastic wrap, and put them in a warm place. Within a few days, the spores collected from the dirt and crumbs will grow and multiply at an amazing rate. Use the magnifying glass to look closely at the molds.

Spore soup is a good science fair project. Try different things to collect the spores: pond water, crumbs of cheese, household dust, and soil are a few ideas.

The Fizz Factor

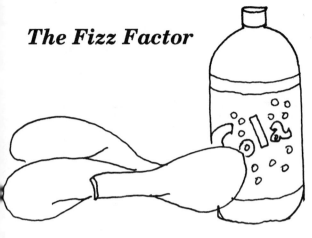

What you will need:

variety of carbonated drinks: root beer, cola, ginger ale, club soda, etc.

balloons: all the same size

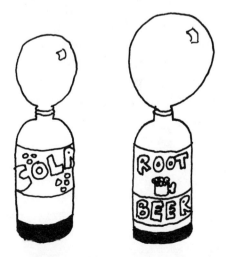

Open the bottles of soda and quickly slip a balloon over the mouth of each bottle. You may have to shake the bottles (with a hand firmly over the balloon) to fully inflate the balloons.

The fizz in carbonated drinks is from carbon dioxide, a gas sealed into the drink and released when the bottle is open. The balloon captures the carbon dioxide and inflates according to the amount of carbonation in the soda.

Experiment! Try different size bottles with different size balloons. Tie off one of the carbon dioxide inflated balloons, and blow up another balloon by mouth. Throw both up into the air and see which lands first, determining which is heavier: carbon dioxide or air.

Sugar Crystals

What child can resist watching candy in the making? This experiment is a good opportunity for introducing young children to the magic of science.

What you will need:

powdered sugar (dissolves easier than plain sugar)

hot water

foil and a dish or a glass, cotton yarn, pencil, and paper clips

Pour 1/4 cup hot water into a small mixing bowl and add enough sugar until absolutely no more will dissolve, approximately 1 cup. There are two ways to form the crystals: 1. Pour the solution into a foil covered dish. 2. Tie two or three lengths of cotton yarn to a pencil, and fasten a paper clip to the other end. Pour the solution into a glass, and place the pencil over the rim of the glass with the weighted yarn in the solution.

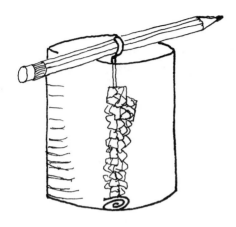 

Several days later, as the water evaporates, you will see the crystal formations on the string or foil. When the solution has evaporated completely, turn out the crystals onto black construction paper, and examine them closely with a magnifying glass.

The water changed the tiny crystals of sugar into larger crystals, without changing their chemical composition. The crystals formed on the string will be even bigger than the ones formed on the dish, because the slower evaporation process allows larger crystals to form.

The Tooth Project

The transformation of a strong, white tooth into a discolored one with cavities is a dramatic reminder to care for our teeth.

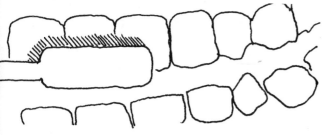

What you will need:

teeth: Ask your dentists for the teeth saved from extractions.

cola

orange juice

vinegar

milk

water: used as a "control" if you have enough teeth

Cola   Milk   Vinegar   H₂O

Clean the collected teeth and examine them with your child. Point out the crown and root, and which teeth are used for grinding versus tearing. This conversation can ramble from dinosaurs ("Which teeth look like a meat eaters'? How about a plant eater's?") to the teeth of animals around the home.

Pour the cola, vinegar, milk, water, and orange juice into separate, small jars and add a tooth. Let your child use his imagination for different solutions to experiment with. We tried mashed up blackberries. The tooth turned an impressive purple-gray that wouldn't wash off.

The results of this project depend on the size and condition of the tooth. The tooth in cola reacts within a few days as the sugar and carbonation break down the enamel and forms pits. The acids in orange juice and vinegar also work against the tooth, but take more time.

The Way Water Travels

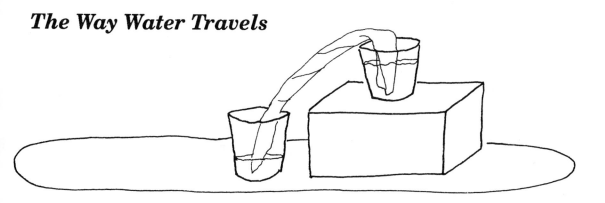

What you will need:

cotton handkerchief or scarf

two glasses

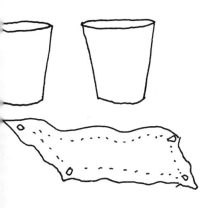

Have your child fill one glass with water, and place it on a small box or an object that will elevate it. Place the empty glass on the table beside it, lower than the filled glass. Roll the scarf into a cylinder and place the ends into the glasses. The water will eventually travel down from the full glass into the empty glass.

Try using a white handkerchief and put a few drops of food coloring in the water. When it fills the empty glass, add a different color to the water. Ask your child to guess what will happen to the handkerchief. (It will take several hours, or overnight, for the water to do its trick.)

Crack Your Marbles

I was waiting at the dentist office beside an interesting ten year-old boy. Our idle conversation roved to what he considered fun, and I asked him what his favorite science experiment was. Crack your marbles!

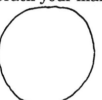 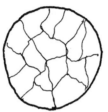

What you will need:

marbles
cookie sheet
ice

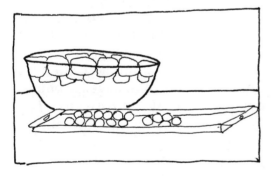

Have your child put the marbles on the cookie sheet, and place them in a 300 degree oven for a half hour. Fill a bucket or sink with cold water and add the ice. Quickly add the hot marbles to the ice water and watch (listen!) to the cracking process.

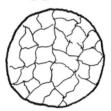 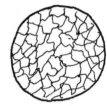

When you heat an object, it expands, and when it cools, it contracts. By cooling the marbles quickly in the ice water, the surface cools faster than the hot center and the glass cracks as a result. If you were to allow the marbles to cool naturally, they wouldn't crack, because the glass molecules cool at the same rate, and stay the same size. What happens when you place some of the hot marbles in hot or tepid water? Experiment!

Balloon Trolley

A toy that travels, a game that teaches. This project is accessible science for even the youngest family member.

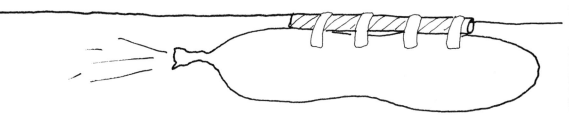

What you will need:
fish line
balloons: different shapes and sizes
tape
straws

Blow up a balloon and hold it closed while your child tapes a straw to the balloon's surface. When using a long skinny balloon, tape two straws in a row.

To make a rail for the trolley, thread the fishline through the straw on the balloon, tie one end to a stationary object such as a fence or pole, and the other end a good distance away. We did this project on our deck, and strung four rails down its length for races.

Blow up the balloon at one end of the rail, and release it. The air rushing out will move the balloon along the line. This propulsion is an important principle for air travel. Talk about how rockets move, and experiment with different size balloons to discover which size travels the longest distance.

Science Shorts

No time for science? These experiments take only a few moments, but provide an important arena for children to explore the environment.

Watch Me Grow

This project is a graphic reminder for children of how quickly their bodies grow. Use an indelible marker, and mark a small spot on the base of your child's fingernail. Cover the mark with clear nail polish for durability, and watch it rise to the top of the finger as the nail grows.

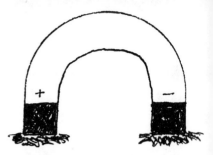

Star Dust

The composition of the earth's crust includes meteor bits that have collided with our planet every day since its creation, leaving a surprising amount of debris on its surface.

It is possible to collect a few of these meteor particles because they are composed of nickel and iron, both substances attracted to a magnet. Have your child drag the magnet along the ground, or at the beach and closely observe the particles it attracts. About twenty per cent of these are meteor pieces.

Sub in a Cup

What you will need:

paper towels
cup

The Needle and Balloon Trick

What you will need:

needle
inflated balloon
transparent tape

Have your child firmly shove a few paper towels into the bottom of the cup. Then overturn the cup and have her evenly push it into the water without tipping the sides. Trapped air is forced upward as the cup is lowered below the surface of the water, keeping the paper towels dry. The old diving bells used this principle for early exploration of the sea.

Place a small piece of tape on the balloon, and press it firmly into place. Poke the needle through the tape and balloon. It doesn't pop! The tape holds the surface of the balloon together, preventing the air from rushing out and tearing the balloon (the tearing is what causes the balloon to pop with a bang). This is a wonderful trick for children to perform before their friends.

OUTDOORS

There is nothing like the combination of a sunny day, children alive with energy, and idle hours waiting to be filled. This chapter of outdoor ideas will take advantage of high spirits and the creative opportunies that nature offers.

A number of the projects require time and patience: for the fruit to grow in a bottle, pumpkins to swell to size, or the response to a cast out message. These projects are an exercise of steady purpose in an age of quick fixes, and can help our families be aware of the side of life that takes time for the longed-for results.

Other projects are meant only for fun: super squirts with their satisfying reach of water, or scarecrow with its dual role of sentinel and clown.

Beach Weaving

The process of slowly weaving a beach's treasures into a wall hanging is a special way to make a memory with your child.

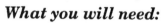

What you will need:

small boards for a frame

small nails

twine

beach grass, driftwood, rope, corks, seaweed, etc.

Go for a walk on the beach to find an interesting piece of driftwood for the top of your weaving. The size of the driftwood, and the length you wish your weaving to be, will determine how big to build your frame.

The frame doesn't need to be fancy. Nail a few boards together in a rectangle, for example, and loosely tie the piece of driftwood to the top of the frame. Nail a row of nails one inch apart at the bottom of the frame, the length of the driftwood.

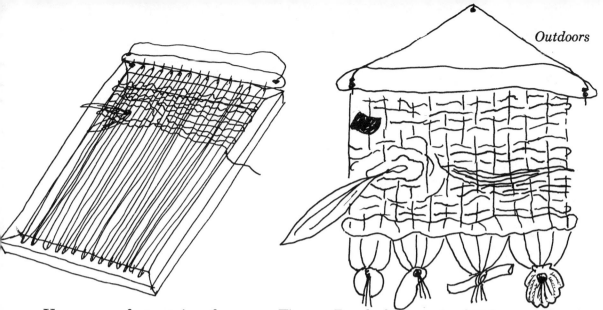

You are ready to string the warp. Tie the twine around the driftwood only and go down to the first nail, hook it with the twine, and back up and around the driftwood. Lift the driftwood up each time you come up from the nails with the twine, and go around it. This will keep it independent from the frame. Continue the stringing with each nail, pulling the twine reasonably taut to form your warp for weaving into. Tie the driftwood firmly to the frame when you are finished.

Ready for weaving? Take your frame to the beach and collect beach grass, feathers, washed up rope, interesting pieces of driftwood, etc. and weave them into the warp with an in-and-out motion. Tamp the weaving material down with your fingers as you go along. Be sure the successive layers are in an opposing in-and-out pattern to get the proper weave. When you are finished, cut the driftwood from the frame, and lift the piece from the nails.

Dried Flowers

There are a number of ways to dry flowers, but the easiest is air drying. To air dry, have your child gather a bouquet and strip the leaves off the stems. Fasten a rubber band or twine near the bottom, and hang upside down where there is good air circulation and not too much light. These bouquets are lovely to look at while drying. I like to use a wooden clothes rack in the kitchen.

KEEP THIS
Borax
and Corn
meal
for flowers

For more perfect looking flowers, dry them in a borax-cornmeal mixture. Have your child mix equal parts of borax (available in the detergent section of the grocery store) and corn meal. Pour a small amount of the mixture in a container, and place the flowers head up. (If you are drying flat petaled flowers such as daisies, place them head down.) Gently stream the mixture over the flowers until they are covered. They may take several days to over a week to dry, depending on the type of flowers. This method produces magnificent flowers with only a slight loss of color.

Dried flower heads make a wonderful addition to potpourri. Keep a large jar full of them during the summer months for making potpourri as gifts for the holidays.

Fruit in a Bottle

Amaze friends with this variation on a ship-in-a-bottle trick!

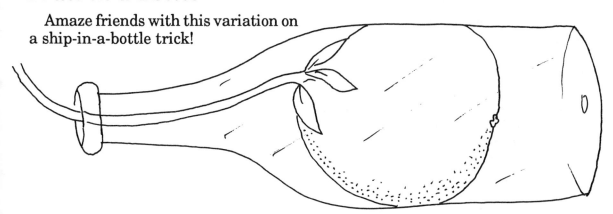

What you will need:

bottle with a small opening: large soda bottle, or an old fashioned milk bottle works fine

tiny green apple, or tomato, cucumber, zuchini, pear, etc.

While the young fruit is still growing on the plant, place it in the bottle, and tie or prop the bottle so it is secure. If you are going to use a tomato, choose one on the stem close to the mother plant. These generally grow biggest. The bottle acts as a greenhouse, and the fruit grows to fill the bottle. When it is ready, snip it off!

Garden Patch

Georgia O'Keefe once said it takes *time* to look at something, and in this age of accelerated lifestyles, it is rare that we take the time to really notice nature's slowly evolving cycles. The waxing and waning of the moon each month, the growth of a seed and its eventual return to the soil, the gentle progression of the seasons are but a few reminders of the natural cycles in our environment.

The progression of seed to plant, to flower and to seed again closely parallels the progressive cycles of all life. Providing a pot or a section of garden to plant in, enables your child to explore this powerful and complete cycle. Don't be inhibited by lack of space or gardening skills. You will learn along with your child what works best.

Go to the nursery together to collect seeds, or better yet, allow some of the flower and vegetables in your garden to seed, and harvest them. They will keep until spring if placed in an envelope or small sealed container, and stored in a cool, dark spot. Let your child decide the types of plants she wants in her garden, and turn her loose in her patch. Even without scientific soil preparation, and neat rows, the vigorous nature of seeds will assert itself and they will produce something.

I found that using the flat peat tablets that pop up in water is an inexpensive and effective way to plant and observe a seed's growth. Try the bigger seeds like sunflowers, nasturtiums, pumpkin, and peas. Place the peat pot in soil when the plant has established itself.

As the garden grows, talk about what is happening. Each season has an effect upon the plant. Spring encourages initial growth; summer provides the warmth necessary for bees to fertilize the flowers; autumn air allows the seeds to cure; and winter breaks down the body of the plant and returns it to the soil.

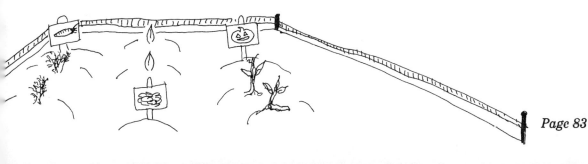

Butterfly Net

You can buy your child a dozen nets over the summer, but none will match the value of this self-constructed tool.

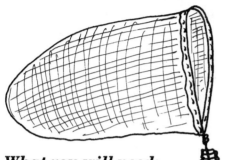

What you will need:

tulle: netting available at your fabric store.

stick: an old broom handle, piece of driftwood, or stick from a tree

coat hanger: pulled into a circle with the hook straightened out

needle and thread

adhesive tape

Cut the tulle into a circle roughly two feet across. Keep in mind the bigger the circle, the bigger the net. We used a garbage can lid as a pattern. Fold the edges of the circle over the rounded hanger. Have your child sew down this hem of net (make it narrow to keep the net size roomy) to attach it to the hanger. Holding the hem over the hanger for your child will make the sewing easier.

Once the net is sewn into place, you are ready to attach it to the stick. Wrap the straightened hook of the hanger near one end of the stick. Tape securely into place. The net is ready! We have used ours not only for butterflies, but also for catching frogs, retrieving balloons from trees, and for an invented game of toss-and-catch with a tennis ball. Have fun!

Garden Paper

A lovely, rough textured paper that varies in color with the plants used.

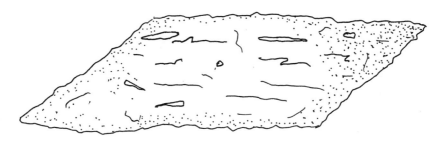

What you will need:

1 cup garden stuff torn into small pieces: grass, flowers, leaves, soft vegetables such as tomatoes or zuchini

1 cup finely shredded paper: tissue, toilet paper, or napkins work best

blender

water

newspapers

screen cut into a 12 inch square (small rolls of screen are available at your hardware store)

wax paper

Place the garden stuff and the shredded paper into a blender, and fill two thirds with water. Blend until the mixture is the texture of mush. Pour into a colander over the sink and drain. Put the screen on a pad of newspapers, and place the drained paper mixture onto the screen. Cover with a sheet of wax paper and roll the pulp out, changing newspapers until the pad is fairly dry on the last roll.

Lift the screen from the newspaper and allow the garden paper to dry. Check the paper after a few hours and lift the edges a little for easier removal later. When it is fully dry, your child can write a poem or draw a picture on it, and you have a unique work of art!

Critter Cage

Every child at one time or another catches a bug or a frog and asks for a jar to keep it in. This is an easy cage to make that allows your child to observe these worthy specimens in larger, more natural conditions. With a little care, you can watch tadpoles grow into frogs, a spider build its web, or a caterpillar spin its cocoon.

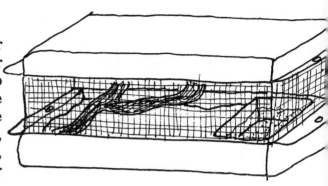

What you will need:

plaster of paris: approximately 3 1/2 cups

screen

2 foil lasagna-sized pans

1 foil casserole pan (single serving size)

For a smaller critter cage:

2 tuna fish cans

screen

plaster of paris

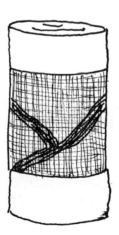

Cut a length of screen twelve inches tall and long enough to fit around the inside edges of the lasagna pan. Bend the screen into the shape of the pan and tape or staple the edges together.

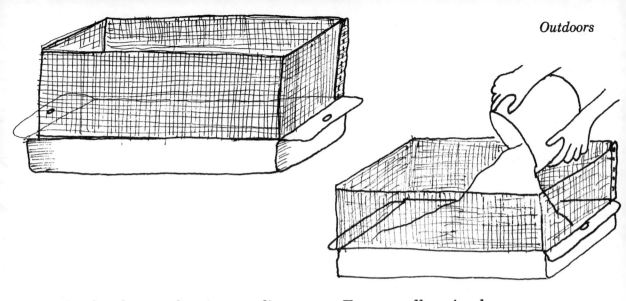

Mix the plaster of paris according to the directions on the package. Put the mixed plaster into the bottom of one lasagna pan, and spread it out evenly. Set the shaped screen into the plaster. Gently press the small casserole pan into one end of the cage; this is your pond. When the plaster dries, you will be able to remove the pond to add water for polliwogs or frogs. The other lasagna pan acts as a lid when placed on top of the cage.

For a smaller, simpler version of a critter cage, roll a piece of screen to fit inside the tuna can, and tape or staple the ends closed. Pour prepared plaster of paris into the can and place the roll of screen in before it sets. Place the other tuna can on top for a lid.

BRANCH   WATER DISH

Beach Glass Mosaic

The search for the water-worn glass is part of the process of these translucent mosaics. They are particularly beautiful hung in windows.

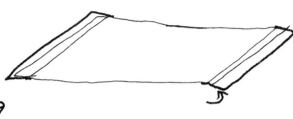

What you will need:

beach glass (the more the better)

pane of glass from an old picture frame (I get mine from thrift shops)

cloth tape (wide and black is best)

household glue

shoe string or leather boot lace for hanging

To prepare for the mosaic, have the children sort the beach glass by color into different dishes. We always include an "unusual" dish for the shells, bits of driftwood, and other unique fruits of the tide that we could not resist.

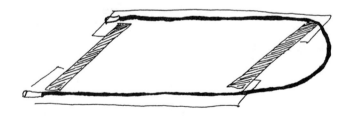

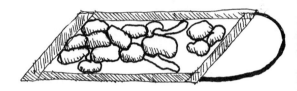

While they are sorting, make a hanger for the mosaic by taping the shoestring or lace onto the sides of the glass, using the cloth tape. Run the lace all the way down both sides of the glass. Make sure you tape the lace securely onto the glass. Frame the top and bottom of the glass with the tape for a finished look. This also protects the edges of the glass against a fall.

The children create the 'picture' they want by gluing the pieces of beach glass onto the framed glass. When the glue is dry, hang the mosaic with a small hook near a window.

Weird and Wonderful Pumpkins

Pumpkins are easy to cultivate. They produce Jack-O-Lanterns for Halloween, make tasty pies, and they are an excellent plant to harvest seeds from to grow the following year. Consider the bush variety for smaller gardens.

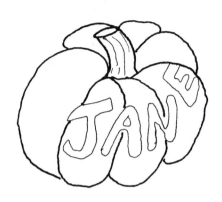

Personal Pumpkins

Have your child write his name onto a green pumpkin with a blunt pencil while the skin is still tender. The scratched out name will fill in with raised brown letters, and personalize the Jack-O-Lantern.

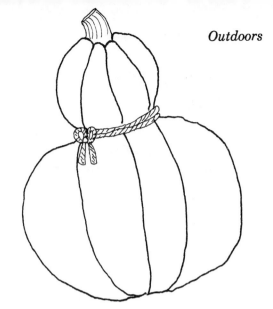

For the Biggest Pumpkin on the Block

Choose a big variety seed, such as Jack-O-Lantern, to plant. When the pumpkins have appeared, select a pumpkin closest to the mother plant, and prune off all the others. When it reaches soccer ball size, carefully slit the stem between the vine and pumpkin, and insert a piece of cotton string into the slit. Leave enough string dangling out to put into a bucket of water. Keep the bucket filled through the growing season and the pumpkin will draw the water directly from the bucket and grow to astonishing proportions.

Pumpkin with a Body

Tie a cord or rope tightly around a green pumpkin while it is still on the vine. The pumpkin will grow around the tie to form a "head" and "body." Experiment with various widths of cord for different results.

Plaster of Paris Sand Casting

I tried this project for the first time on a sizzling afternoon. The sand was too hot for this project, and the plaster set nearly as fast I poured. Pick a day for the beach when the sand is temperate.

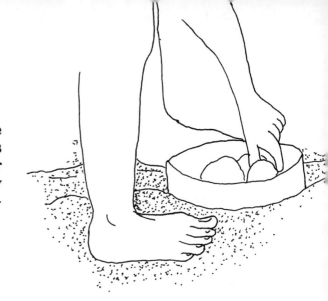

What you will need:

plaster of paris

plastic bucket

collars cut from flexible cardboard to make the frame: 2 to 3 inches wide and stapled into a circle

cup

paper clips or wire for hanging the plaques

spoon or stick to stir the plaster

Have the children collect their beach treasures for the plaques while you scout for a level, sandy place for the casting. Push the collars into the sand.

There are two ways to make the plaques. If your child wants to spend time arranging the shells, place them into the sand within the collar frame before pouring the plaster. If she wants to design quickly, pour the plaster into the collar first, and arrange the treasures on top.

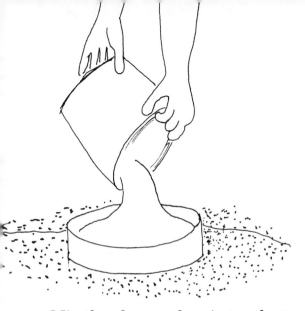

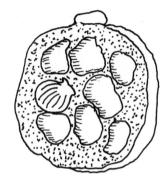

Mix the plaster of paris to a batter consistency using sea water. Work fairly fast, particularly if you are making several plaques. Pour the plaster into the collars over the beach treasures, or arrange the treasures on top. While the plaster is still wet, insert the paper clips or wire that will serve as hangers. Another popular but special design idea is to press your child's hand or foot into the plaster after it has firmed up a bit.

The hardening time varies with the warmth of the sand, the day's humidity, and the consistency of the plaster. Plan on 5 to 30 minutes.

To Build a Scarecrow

Whether or not you have a garden is unimportant. A scarecrow not only wards off big black crows from a garden, but also appeals to children as a protective shaman on their turf.

What you will need:

old white pillowcase for the head

2x2 board, 6 feet long (ask the lumberyard to make a point on one end)

1x4 board, 3 to 4 feet long for the arms (proportions are approximate, lumberyards usually have scrap heaps you can peruse)

old clothes, including hat or wig

stuffing: straw, dried leaves, or rags work fine

nails and twine

Nail the 3 foot board onto the longer board about a foot from the top. This is the body frame which can be used year after year. Pull an old shirt over the arms, and slip a leg from a pair of pants through the long board, or use a skirt for a woman scarecrow. Tuck the shirt inside the pants or skirt, and tie securely with twine.

You are now ready for stuffing. Push the straw or leaves into the shirt body and pants. Pack the pillow case halfway and gather it together to see where to draw the face with an indelible marker or fabric paints. Secure the head with a rubber band or twine and fit it onto the frame. Dig a hole for your scarecrow and place the point in to the ground. Pack the hole with soil and rocks, and tamp it down.

For the final touches, add a hat or wig, tie on a pair of shoes, and pin gardening gloves or mittens at the ends of the sleeves. You can tie pie plates onto the arms to make them clatter and wave in the wind, or loop buckets of fresh flowers for a special effect.

Spore Prints

A project that requires a leisurely walk in spring or autumn. Children are born observers and, if given the time, absorb more information about their environment in a few moments outdoors than they do over hours spent in the classroom.

What you will need:

mushrooms

dark or light construction paper (depending upon the color of the spores)

hair spray

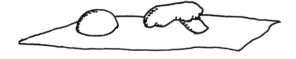

Mushrooms seed themselves with spores that drop from their gills in strange and graceful patterns. To make a print of these patterns, carefully place the mushrooms gathered on your walk, gill side down, on a piece of construction paper. The color of the gills generally indicates the color of the spores. Pick out the shade of construction paper that contrasts best.

It takes several hours for the spores to drop. Leave the mushrooms undisturbed for the most effective pattern. When they have finished dropping their spores, *lightly* spray the print with hair spray.

Underwater Magnifyer

The better to see those frog eggs or sea urchins! With this project your child will make a valuable tool to observe the ponds, puddles, and tide pools of her world.

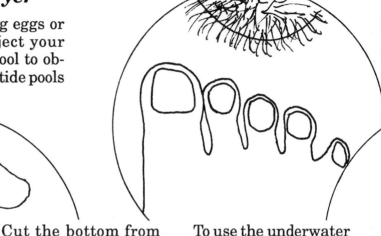

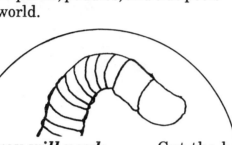

What you will need:

plastic bucket or a plastic gallon jug that holds restaurant condiments, usually free for the asking

plastic wrap

large rubber band

Cut the bottom from the plastic bucket or jug. Take a piece of plastic wrap, and lay it across the end with a ridge. Place the rubber band over the plastic wrap to hold it into place.

To use the underwater magnifyer, lower it into the water and observe. The pressure of the water pushing into the wrap, forms a concave magnifying lens that enlarges the things your child is looking at.

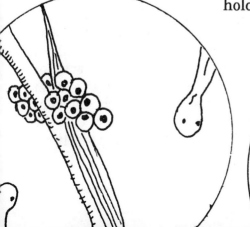

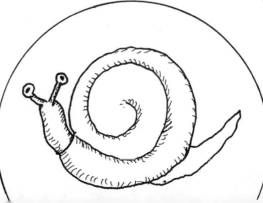

Solar Prints

An inexpensive process for beautiful prints, using the sun's energy.

What you will need:

blueprint paper: available at office or art supply stores

ammonia

tray or board

large bottle with tight fitting lid: the large, glass ones restaurants use for condiments work well

objects to print: hands, feathers, fern leaves, household objects, etc.

In a room without much light, cut the large sheets of blueprint paper into smaller pieces. Roll them back up and slip the sheets into a dark plastic bag. When your child is finished gathering the objects for printing, go outdoors with the remaining materials.

Pour a small amount of ammonia (3 or 4 tablespoons) into the large bottle and tightly cap the lid. Take out a sheet of paper, and place it on the tray or board. Work fairly fast once the sheet of blue print paper is out of the bag, but don't rush the artist too much. Use the first print as a test and take your time.

Nest Pickings

What makes a nest? You may be surprised!

What you will need:

onion bag, or any wide-webbed bag

wire hanger

nest pickings: foil, feathers, leaves, straw, yarn, cotton, small twigs, moss, strips of fabric, hair, wool, etc.

Have your child lay the objects for printing upon the paper, and expose it to the sun for a few minutes. There will be a *slight* change of color to the paper with the exposure to the sun, but nothing dramatic until you remove the objects, drop the blueprint paper, unfolded, into the jar with the ammonia, and replace the lid. The fumes of the ammonia act as a "developer," and there is an immediate change as the shaded areas from the objects turn a deep blue. Remove the paper from the jar when the print looks ready.

Have your child pull the hanger into a diamond. Cut a small hole at the tope of the onion bag for the top of the hanger to slip through, and weave the nest pickings into the webbing of the bag. Hang it outdoors in the spring and watch the birds choose their nest materials.

Let's Build Boats!

I can tell you how to build a dynami-
cally sound milk-carton boat, a sailboat
with balloon pontoons, or a snazzy
catamaran, but you will never know
the profound joy of watching a budding
engineer at work unless you turn a
child loose with the right materials and
an idea: Let's build boats!

What you will need:

*styrofoam plates, cups,
trays*

*tape (plastic tape works
best in water)*

straws (the bending kind)

*balloons, long skinny ones
and round ones*

pipe cleaners

milk cartons

bamboo skewers

sponges

egg cartons

popsicle sticks

fish bobbers, fishing line

corks

paper or plastic for sails

string

wood scraps

nails

foil

Clear a table for your
boat building materials,
and while the children
are busy inventing, you
can, if you wish, build
one of the following more
conventional boats. Your
child may follow your
project at first and then
take off on a variation.

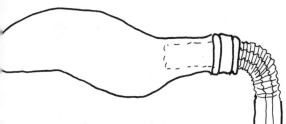

Catamaran

Tape two styrofoam or plastic cups together for a pontoon, repeat for the other side, and tape the pontoons onto a styrofoam meat tray. Make a sail with paper, thread it onto a bamboo skewer, and poke it onto the tray. You can also inflate long skinny balloons for the pontoons, or use a round balloon for the sail: just poke a hole in the tray, and the knot will hold the balloon in place.

Traditional Milk Carton Boat

This never-fail boat design includes deep pontoons for carrying cargo. Use either a quart or half gallon size carton. Pick a corner and with a sharp knife slice down the fold. Continue diagonally across the bottom and top of the carton, but do not cut the opposing corner (see diagram). You will have a marvelously seaworthy vessel. We used a bamboo skewer threaded onto a styrofoam plate for a sail, but you can also experiment with paper, cloth, or balloon sails.

Power Boat

Tape a good sized round balloon (the bigger the balloon, the farther your boat will go) close to the bending part of a flexible straw. Make sure the balloon is attached securely enough that you can inflate it using the straw. For the body of the boat, cut a styrofoam plate in half, trim 2 inches from both halves, and tape the plate back together. Poke a hole near the stern of your boat and insert the straw with the balloon part up for the sail. Blow up the balloon, and when you're ready for launching, release and watch it go!

Message in a Bottle

Casting out a message in a bottle is experiencing expectation in it fullest sense. It is an easy project that demonstrates tidal and current patterns, and the ingredients are simple: a bottle with a cap or cork, a message inside, and a body of water to throw it in.

There are a number of factors that will influence the course of your bottle, such as launch location, wind, and indigenous currents and tides.

Twice a month the sun and moon align and pull together, and the resulting tides are higher. This occurs when the moon is full, and two weeks later at the new moon. These higher than average tides each month are called spring tides, and it may help to take advantage of them to launch your bottle.

Another important factor is location. You can throw it from a ferry, a beach, a bridge, or a boat, with equally good results. Not all bottles will be found, and no matter how carefully you take all the factors into consideration, it still remains to chance that someone discovers your message. Don't let this stop you. Every child can use disappointment to develop resiliency for facing challenges.

This project is a worthy science fair project for older children. Try throwing several bottles out in different locations, and keep a journal of the weather, tides, and conditions of each launching. Good luck!

Water Dredge

This easy-to-make water dredge collects the rich life living near the bottom of the beach, a pond, or the backyard puddle. A book from the library on water creatures and plants will help identify your child's treasures.

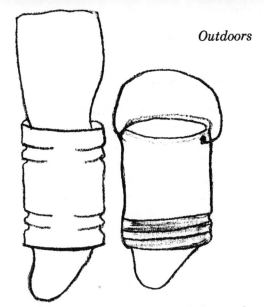

What you will need:

- *coffee can: one 1 lb. size, with both top and bottom taken out*
- *old nylon stocking*
- *adhesive tape*
- *corkscrew or hammer and nail*
- *coat hanger with the hook snipped off, and the wire straightened*

Have your child slip the nylon stocking over the opened can, leaving some stocking at the bottom for the dredge collection. Gather the extra nylon around the top of the can.

To make a sturdy handle for the dredge, use the cork screw or the hammer and nail to pierce holes on opposite sides of the can. Thread the coat hanger wire through the holes and nylon, and bend the ends up to hold into place. Tape the excess stocking down and around the can.

To use the dredge, drag it by the handle near the bottom of a pond. The water will drain off while the collected specimen concentrate at the bottom in the stocking. Have a bucket handy to hold the contents of the collection for studying at home.

Super Squirts

I could sense with mother radar things were getting out of hand outside. Underneath the noise of a half dozen playing kids, was the high pitched sound of unabridged excitement, the kind of excitement that heralds the entry of something new on the scene, something to be hidden. I went out to investigate. Soaking wet children appeared and disappeared and my walk turned into a march.

I came upon our 13 year-old neighbor squirting the laughing targets with a powerful jet of water. "Mead!..." I began, and stopped as he turned around. He had a weird thing wrapped around his body. It appeared to be a four foot sausage filled with water, and with a flick of his hand, a twenty foot line of wet shot out. Overcome with curiosity, I asked him what it was. Using surgical tubing and the bottom of a ball point pen for a nozzle, he had fashioned a squirt gun to rival any high tech toy on the market.

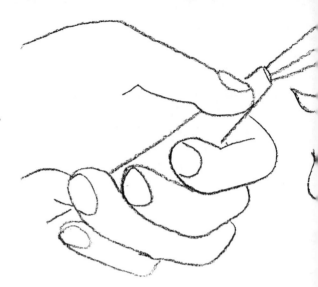

It wasn't much of a decision. I skipped the scolding and asked him to show me how he made it. The next day we bought the tubing and made a half dozen in a few minutes. I filled mine first as everyone crowded around. The tubing stretched out magically and grew heavy with water. With something like that in your hands, you *have* to squirt someone. I turned on the kids gleefully, and for good measure squirted my friend, too. Thank you, Mead Trick, for sharing one of the most fun water projects we have tried!

Cut the tubing to the length desired, and knot one end. The ball point pen half fits snugly into the opposite end for a nozzle. Securely tape it into place. There's your super squirt! The trick now is to fill it. We found that the narrow mouth on a brass sweeper nozzle made it easy.

Fill the super squirt slowly by pressing the opening of the pen head into the sweeper nozzle and turning on the water. The pressure of the entering water will cause the tubing to expand like a water balloon. The longer the super squirt, the farther the stream will travel. To stop the stream, simply cover the pen opening with a finger. Be sure to make one for yourself and join the fun!

What you will need:

3/8" surgical tubing, availabe by the foot at hardware stores

ballpoint pen half: the pointed end

tape: electrical or duct works well

brass water sweeper nozzle: available at hardware stores

PRESENTS

Handmade presents for those we love, for friends, teachers, or the school bus driver, resonate long after we give them simply because the investment is not money but self. The making of a gift is evidence of heart and hands at work, and the process offers children the chance to experience the rich joy of giving.

Not every child will be in a gift-making mood however, when a birthday or holiday demands it. Take advantage of creative moments and keep a box year round for the gifts your family makes.

Make Your Own Book

This project is easier than it sounds, and the result is something to be proud of.

What you will need:

2 pieces of cardboard for the covers

fabric pieces to cover cardboard

needle and thread (or sewing machine to sew pages together)

cloth tape (available at hardware stores)

paper for the pages

strip of cardboard for the spine

decorated paper to be used as endpapers

Fold three to five sheets of paper in half (we found it easiest to use 8"x11" sheets) and sew along the fold line by hand or with a sewing machine. Each set of folded papers is called a signature. Your child's book may need several signatures before she considers it ready. To put the signatures together, run a little glue along a folded edge of each group

and press together under something heavy until dry.

Lay the cardboard over a piece of fabric, fold the corners in as shown in the diagram, and glue the fabric down. Don't worry about covering the cardboard entirely: you will use a decorated endpaper to cover the inside of the cover later. Repeat for the back cover.

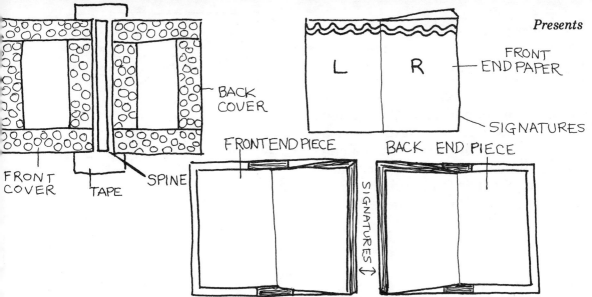

FRONT END PAPER

SIGNATURES

BACK COVER

FRONT COVER

TAPE

SPINE

L   R

FRONT END PIECE

BACK END PIECE

SIGNATURES

SIGNATURES ↔

Now you are ready to make the spine. Place the inside edge of the covers on a piece of cloth tape cut long enough to fold over the top and bottom generously. Space the covers so you can place the strip of cardboard between them for the spine. Fold tape ends over the spine.

The next step is to place the signatures in the center of the spine. Spread glue over a decorated endpaper,* folded in half, and glue half of the end paper to the signatures and the other half onto the cover (see diagram). Do this to both front and back cover and signatures.

The endpapers hold the signatures into the book, and they will be loose against the spine, just like in a real book. Make sure your signatures are completely dry before glueing them to the endpapers.

Now that the book is finished, there are many ways to use it: as a journal, an address book, a place to keep ideas or write a story. Offer to write down a dictated story, secretary style, even for children who write. This releases them from the time-consuming task of forming letters when their imagination is active.

(*see Marbelized Paper)

Bath Powder

The beauty of this project is in the mixing of the ingredients. Cornstarch has a special "feel" to it, and makes a natural powder. Bring your child along when you pick out the oil. There are dozens to choose from, and smelling them all is an experience in itself.

What you will need:

cornstarch

essential oil or perfume oil (available at many bath shops specializing in perfume and potpourri)

tin to hold the powder, and powder puff (available in drug stores)

or:

a large fancy salt shaker

For every half cup of constarch, add approximately 10 drops of oil, and mix well with your hands. Place the powder in the salt shaker, or in the tin with the powder puff. These are fun birthday gifts to make for friends, too.

Homemade Beads

The texture of this dough and its ability to absorb color, combine to yield uncommonly beautiful beads. Plan on making several batches of different colors.

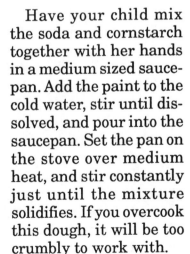

What you will need:

1 cup baking soda

1/2 cup cornstarch

tempera paint for coloring the dough (Tubes of water color, fabric dye, and food coloring also work well.)

3/4 cup cold water

Have your child mix the soda and cornstarch together with her hands in a medium sized saucepan. Add the paint to the cold water, stir until dissolved, and pour into the saucepan. Set the pan on the stove over medium heat, and stir constantly just until the mixture solidifies. If you overcook this dough, it will be too crumbly to work with.

When the dough cools, knead it until smooth and pliable. You are now ready to make beads! There are dozens of ways to do this, but leave it to your child to discover the best one. You can free form the beads into shapes with your hands, or roll snakes from the dough to cut with a knife.

After the dough is shaped into a bead, poke a toothpick down the center to form a hole for stringing. If the holes are big enough, a shoestring works beautifully for small hands to string the beads. Older children can make smaller holes and string the beads with fishing line.

Grapefruit Bowl

These bowls dry to a hard, gourd-like finish, making perfect containers for potpourri or other little treasures.

What you will need:

grapefruit or orange, thick skinned is best

grapefruit knife (blunt, serrated knife with an angled end)

metal jar lid rings, or some other form for the fruit to dry around

Cut across the grapefruit one third down from the top. This makes a bowl and lid. The next step is a good opportunity for your child to work with a relatively safe knife. Have him run the knife around the inside of the fruit, making it easier to scrape or pull the pulp from the walls of the skin down to the white pulp.

Insert the metal rings inside the scraped out lid and bowl to help the fruit retain its shape. Experiment with molding the fruit skin with a jar, cookie cutter, anything that holds the walls while it dries.

There are two ways to dry the bowls: air drying which takes longer but dries more uniformly, or drying slowly in a 200 degree oven.

Fish Prints

Art from the fish that didn't get away. These prints look beautiful framed, and are a good example of using a familiar product in a completely different way.

What you will need:

fish (it's fun to use weird ones like carp)

water soluble ink

paper (typing paper is fine; rice paper is better)

brayer (roller to spread ink)

Have your child rinse the fish, pat it dry, and lay it on a cookie sheet. Squirt some ink in a flat dish and roll the brayer back and forth across it to cover the ink roller. Roll the ink-covered brayer over the fish until the face-up side is covered with ink; don't forget the fins, which sometimes lay flat against the body.

Gently place the paper over the fish, and lightly rub the paper with the palm of your hand. Peel off the paper and there it is, a beautiful fish print!

Pomanders

Pomanders have a glorious fragrance, make wonderful gifts, and are easy enough for even young children to make.

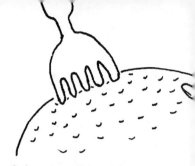

What you will need:

apples, lemons, limes, or oranges, firm and thin skinned

whole cloves

fork

spices to cure: cinnamon, nutmeg, allspice

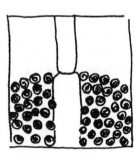

There are a few simple rules for pomanders: it is easier to insert the cloves if you prick the fruit with a fork first, and for it to keep well, the cloves should be placed fairly close together. However, don't worry about the fruit keeping well if your child is intent upon his design. If you want to hang the pomander, leave a trail around the fruit the size of the ribbon you will be using. This makes a handy groove to hold it in place.

When you've finished putting the cloves into the fruit, cure the pomander with the spices. Have your child mix the spices in a large shallow dish. The amount needed depends upon how many pomanders you are curing. Swish the pomanders around in the spice mixture until they are well coated, then leave them in the dish until they harden. This may take from two weeks to a month, depending on the type of fruit used.

Seed Cards

Fun "living"cards for birthdays. Keep in mind that a single layer of seeds will grow much better than piles.

What you will need:

sponge
seeds: grass, alfalfa, bird seed, etc.

Have your child cut the sponge into an interesting shape, number, or letter, or leave it in a rectangle so the seeds can make the shape. Dampen the cut sponge and dip onto a plate sprinkled with the seeds, or sprinkle the seeds into the desired shape. Place the seed card on a tray and keep moist until the sprouts begin to grow.

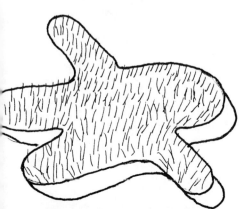

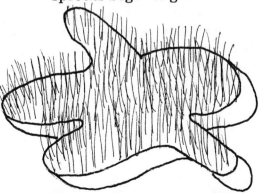

Potpourri

This project is simple, but takes time. As my children waited for their flower petals to dry, I realized how much emphasis we place on immediate results and yet how rewarding it can be to wait patiently for something special. With potpourri, the fruit of summer is yours year round.

The following ingredients are ideas for your child's potpourri. You can provide any or all of them, or add your own. Children can collect and dry the flowers themselves by scattering whole heads or the petals in a single layer on a newspaper, and placing them in an out-of-the-way place. Leave the petals until thoroughly dry (a week or longer), then pack them in one-inch layers in a large jar, topping each layer thickly with iodized salt. Leave the jar uncovered for several days, then seal tightly until ready to use.

To make the potpourri, place the chosen ingredients in bowls on a table. Encourage your child to smell each one before deciding which would be best for his mix, then have him toss the selected ingredients in a large bowl lightly with his fingers, like an aromatic salad.

The secret to a strong smelling potpourri is essential or perfume oil. Add several drops to the finished potpourri and toss again. Place the potpourri in a covered jar and let it cure for two weeks in a dark place. Display in shells, baskets, bowls, and gourds, or fill tulle (net) circles for sachets.

What you will need:

cloves (whole and ground)

cinnamon

dried yarrow flower heads

bay leaves

nutmeg (ground and whole)

dried lavender

dried mint

cardamom seeds

anise seeds, or stars

allspice

chamomile tea (bulk, not tea bags)

dried flower petals: Dry on newspapers in a single layer until the texture of corn flakes.

dried basil, thyme, rosemary, sage

dried lemon verbena leaves

cedar shavings

vanilla beans

pine snippets

essential or perfume oil: available at bath shops specializing in soaps or perfumes

dried oranges, satsuma, tangerine or lemon peel

Sachets

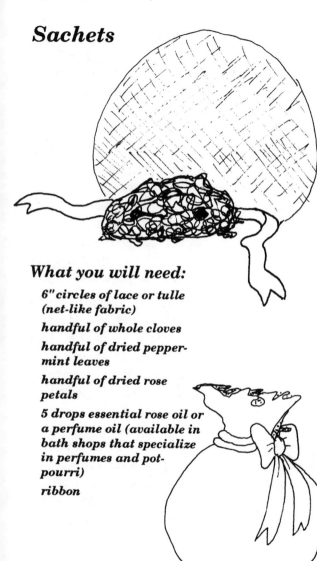

What you will need:

6" circles of lace or tulle (net-like fabric)

handful of whole cloves

handful of dried pepper-mint leaves

handful of dried rose petals

5 drops essential rose oil or a perfume oil (available in bath shops that specialize in perfumes and pot-pourri)

ribbon

Have your child mix the cloves, rose petals, and peppermint leaves in a bowl with his hands. Add the essential or perfume oil, and toss again. The oil will make the sachet scent stronger and last longer, but it is optional. Place a small amount of the mixture in the center of the lace circle, and gather the edge up to tie with a ribbon. Sachets are great favors for children to make at parties.

Marbelized Paper

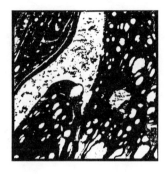

What you will need:

cookie sheet

foil

oil-based paint

typing paper

turpentine (not the pure gum spirit turpentine)

aprons or old shirts to wear

Work in a well ventilated area. Turpentine vapors are strong.

Prepare the paint by thinning it with the turpentine to the consistency of milk. We use small jars with lids for this, to store the unused paint for later use. (I guarantee you will be asked to do this project over!)

Cover the work area with newspapers, and line the cookie sheet with foil. Fill the cookie sheet halfway with water, and have your child dribble drops of the thinned paint onto the water with a small paint brush. The paint may seem to disperse to nothingness on the water's surface at first, but keep adding the drops of paint until it begins to glob.

Swirl the paint around with a pencil or popsicle stick for the marbelized effect, then gently lay a piece of typing paper upon the surface of water. Lift the paper and lay on a newspaper to dry.

Explain to your child that the reason for the marbled look on the paper is that oil and water don't mix together. The oil-based paint is lighter than water and rests on the water's surface. The typing paper acts as a blotter to absorb the swirled paint, and captures the beautiful patterns.

KEEPSAKES

Family vacations, a log of a typical day in the life of the family, the first day of school, are the small parts that make up the fabric of collective family memory. Remembering an event or a shared laugh is a healing and connective process with no rules. We each have unique perspectives on the small and the significant events that shape us into the people we are today.

The following projects involve your children in preserving a moment in the family's life. Their words beneath a photograph, on a cassette tape, or buried in a time capsule are evidence of their own perspective and will provide the rich stuff of memory in years to come.

Time Capsule

A time capsule is a treasure box that preserves the past. We will remember the big events—the exciting trips, the new baby, the big fish that got away—but we tend to forget the smaller features of family life. The routines that shape our days, the school papers, the size of our child's hand, the family's favorite foods, take on a special significance when examined twelve months later. A time capsule captures these priceless details and helps to give a child a sense of passing time, a slippery concept even for adults.

If you plan on burying your time capsule outdoors, you will need a waterproof container: a plastic tub with a lid, or a large jar works well. You may also use an old lunch box, or a cardboard box sealed in a knotted plastic bag.

The afternoon we put our time capsule together, I asked the children to tell me the best and worst part of their day. I wrote this down beside their name and put it in an envelope. We also added individual lists of "Things I am Good At," as well as school papers, drawings, and one special toy apiece. Your child can write a letter to himself, outline feet and hands, or describe dreams, ideas, and favorite pastimes. Height and weight measurements can also be included for comparison when you dig up the capsule.

Seal your treasures in a plastic bag, and place in the container. Bury the capsule in a secret place, or hide it in the house, garage, or attic. You and your family can decide when your capsule should be retrieved. Given a child's rate of development, even a few months may be long enough.

Seasonal Scrapbook

Everyone enjoys reading collected memorabilia about themselves. Whether it is a baby book, scrapbook or photo album, it is always fun to look and remember.

Provide an empty scrapbook and tell your child it is to fill with things about himself. It is helpful to name the book to give it a focus: school days, a favorite sport, animal, hobby, or talent are a few ideas. If presented at the end of the school year, call it a summer scrapbook, and suggest he enter his height and weight for comparison in the autumn. Your child can include tickets, photos, a description of his favorite summer day, lists of books read, friends who spent the night, and trips taken.

Encourage art, poetry, and description on the pages, but realize if it is a book of nothing but horses cut from magazines, it still tells a story about your child from his own authentic point of view.

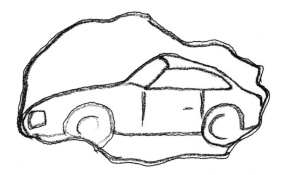

Photo Journal

Photos of the aftermath of a mud fight, the first fish of the season, or lazy days at the beach need not be technically perfect to give rise to a distinct feeling or mood, and that's the secret to this project.

What you will need:

photographs of a vacation, an event, or an important moment for your child

posterboard: 7"x11" size pages

clear contact paper

binding rings

paper punch

It is important your child selects the photos. It is surprising how often that off-centered, discardable photo is the one that speaks to him. Glue the photos near the top of the poster board, leaving plenty of room to write below.

If your child is old enough to write, provide a pen or pencil and let him find the words that tell the story of the photo. Try not to prompt or guide. Writing is an intimate and powerful tool that needs uncensored practice.

this is mom at Lake Centipede

Our new T.V.

If your child is too young to write, sit down and look at the photo together. Ask what she would like to say about the picture and write it down for her. If your child is at a loss for words, talk about how happy she looks in the photo, or how big the sand castle is.

For each page of photo and text, cut a piece of contact paper big enough to seal the sheet front and back. This protects the pages of the book and gives them a finished look. Punch holes down the side for the binding rings, and slip the page through the rings. Your child can also design a cover and back for her journal.

A framed page of the photo journal makes a unique gift for grandparents or, hung on the wall of your home, serves as a daily reminder of those special fleeting moments of childhood.

MY PHOTO JOURNAL SUMMER '89

Art Exhibit

Children's art is a spontaneous and unaffected expression of their world. Encouraging this expression not only develops their creativity but documents a stage in their development. One way to validate children's art is to showcase it with an exhibit, and that is what this project is all about.

One of the most important elements for a successful show is to plan the exhibit well in advance. You may want to exhibit the work of only one child, or make it a neighborhood event for all the children on the block. You may already have a body of your child's art work to exhibit, but if not, consider how much time your family will need to give scope to the art, and allow the really fine ideas a chance to evolve. Keep a special drawer or file for the exhibit. Include poetry, story pictures, crafts, photos, and sculpture.

To make the art exhibit distinctive, you and the children can matte the drawings and paintings on construction paper. Give the special pieces a more professional look by framing them with a mat and glueing this on foam core board (available at art supply or frame shops). While mounting the art for the show, ask if the child wants to title the art pieces.

Every exhibit needs a brief "About the Artist" sketch. Glue a photo of the child on a 7"x11" piece of posterboard, and ask him to describe himself.

TITLE: THE PLUG
MEDIUM: CRAYON
DATE: MAR. 3
THIS IS ONE OF MR.
MAXWELL'S EARLY
PLUG SERIES

SAMUEL ALEX MAXWELL

ABOUT THE ARTIST:
BORN: JULY 1, 1985 226
FAVORITE COLOR: RED
FAVORITE CANDY: TOOTSIE
ROLLS
LIKES TO WEAR BLACK
SWEAT PANTS

YOU ARE INVITED TO AN EXHIBIT OF FINE ART

Once you choose a date for the show, make the invitations. One fun way is to buy blank postcards at the post office or an office supply store and have the children decorate them. Or illustrate a piece of paper with the details of the show, and photo copy it.

Consider making the art exhibit an open house for a few hours so everyone doesn't arrive at once. If there will be poetry or books on display, consider having an informal "reading" by the authors. You will also want to include refreshments made by the children, of course!

One last point: a successful exhibit is informal. This involves the children at every stage of preparation for the show and makes it their own. Let them hang the art where they want, for example. One child's art exhibit roved from bedroom to bathroom to living room, hung on ironing boards and stair railings. It was fully her show, and a testament to the unchecked exuberance of a creative child.

Radio Show

This is a wonderful rainy day activity that can include family and friends. Provide a tape player that your child can operate and a blank cassette. Brainstorm ideas with the children involved: music, interviews, a play, sound effects for a haunted house, or telling jokes and riddles are a few ideas. A simple interview of all the members of the household about likes, dislikes, interests, a typical day, etc., makes a marvelous record of a particular time in the life of the family. Remember to have the children give the date at the beginning or end of each tape.

Adult participation can make the children self-conscious, so after the brainstorming session resist the urge to watch the show in the making, and enjoy the fruits of their labor afterwards!

This is also an excellent way to provide a record of a family trip. Take the tape cassette in the car and encourage the children to keep a daily journal, including distance travelled, places they stayed and interesting sites.

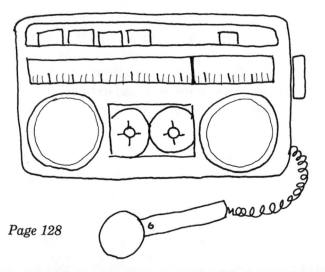

A

Apple turkeys 44
Art exhibit, 126-127

B

Baked bread birthday crown, 35
Ball, super, 4
Balloon
  and needle trick, 75
  inside out, 62
  trolley, 73
Balloons
  CO2 in, 67
Banana pops, chocolate, 22
Bath
  art, 2-3
  powder, 110
Batik egg, dyed, 48-49
Beach
  glass mosaic, 88-89
  projects, 78-79; 88-89; 92-93; 97; 102-103
  weaving, 78-79
Beads, handmade, 111
Bean brawn: weight lifting contest, 54-55
Beeswax candles, 51
Birds, nest materials for, 99
Birthday crown, baked bread, 35
Birthdays
  see Celebrations
Bleaching bones, 8
Boats, building, 100-101
Bone pictures, 8
Bones, rubber, 64
Book, make your own, 108-109
Bottled hurricane, 56
Bubble solution, 2
Bug collecting & viewing, 84; 86; 97; 103
Build a scarecrow, 94-95
Butterfly net, 84

C

Candle lantern, 12
Candles,
  beeswax, 51
  Carbon dioxide
  cannon, 57
  in balloons, 67
Cards
  see Gift cards
Catamaran, 100
Ceiling planetarium, 63
Celebrations, 33-51
 Chocolate
  banana pops, 22
  pudding fingerpaint, 22
  white snowmen, 31
Christmas ornaments, 47
Cinnamon dough mobile, 10
Coffee can
  gingerbread cookies, 21
  ice cream, 23
Coloring flowers, 58
Constructs,
  chicken bone, 8
  marshmallow, 28
  straw and pipecleaner, 7
  vegetable, 20
Cookies
  decorated, 21; 30; 46
  edible holiday cards, 46
  gingerbread coffee can, 21
  stained glass, 30
Cornstarch dough, 111
Crack your marbles, 72
Crayon
  art, 16; 17
  soap, 2
Critter cage, 86-87
Crystals, growing sugar, 68-69

D

Dancing Raisins, 59
Doggie donuts, 29
Dough,
  cinnamon, 10
  cookie, 21; 30; 46
  cornstarch, 111
  gingerbread, 21; 46
  pretzel, 26-27
  salt, 14-15
Dried flowers, 80; 116-117
Drinking straw constructs, 7
Dyes, natural for eggs, 48-50

E

Easter egg extravaganza, 48-49
Easy holiday window decorations, 45
Easy projects
  see Quick and easy projects
Edible art, 19-31
  see also Apple turkeys, 44
  Sugar cube art, 5
  Edible holiday cards, 46
Egg
  dyeing, 48-50
  in a bottle, 60-61
Experiments
  see Science projects

F

Fast stamp from foot padding, 9
Fingerpaint, chocolate pudding, 22
Fish prints, 113
Fizz factor, 67
Float soap, 3
Flowers,
  coloring, 58
  dried, 80, 116-117
Frosting, decorator, 46

Fruit
  flavored stamps, 5
  in a bottle, 81

G

Garden
  paper, 85
  patch, 82-83
Gardening projects, 81-83; 90-91; 94-95
Geo-art boards, 17
Ghost Halloween decoration, 39
Gift cards and stationery, 9; 11; 14-16; 38; 46; 85; 115
Gifts
  see Presents
Gingerbread cookies, 21; 46
Grapefruit bowl, 112

H

Halloween
  costume, 40
  decorations, 39; 41; 45
Hammer and nail project, 17
Handmade
  beads, 111
  soap, 3
  paper, 85
Hands On!, 1-17
Holiday decorations, 5; 10; 30-31; 33-51
Hurricane in a bottle, 56

I

Ice cream in a coffee can, 23
Insects, collecting
  see Bug collecting and viewing
Inside out balloon, 62

K

Keepsakes, 121-128

L

Lantern, tin can, 12

M

Magnifier, underwater, 97
Maps, 3-D, salt dough, 14-15
Marbles, cracking, 72
Marbelized paper, 119
Marshmallow project, 28
Marzipan art, 24
Mask making, 42
Message in a bottle, 102
Milk carton boat, 101
Mobile, 10
Molds, growing, 66
Mushrooms
  see Spore prints

N

Natural dyes for eggs, 48-50
Needle and balloon trick, 75
Nest pickings, 99

O

Onion skin egg dye, 48-49
Outdoor projects, 77-105

P

Paper
  handmade, 85
  marbelized, 119
  tube party favors, 34
Party activity ideas, 21; 23; 33-51; 118
Peanut butter, make your own, 25
Pennies, shine your, 65
Pet treat, 29
Photo journal, 124-125
Pinata, 36-37
Pipecleaner constructs, 7

Planetarium, 36
Plaster of paris sand casting, 92-93
Plaster tape masks, 42-43
Pomanders, 114
Pond life, collecting, 84; 97; 103
Potpourri, 80; 116-117
Power boat, 101
Presents, 3; 21; 38; 51; 80; 88; 107-119; 124-125
Pretzels, 26-27
Printmaking
  fish, 113
  foot padding stamp, 9
  solar, 98
  spore, 96
  styrofoam, 11
Pumpkins
  biggest, 91
  growing, 90-91
  personalized, 90
  with a body, 91

Q

Quick and easy projects
  Apple turkeys, 44
  Bubble solution, 2
  Carbon dioxide cannon, 57
  Chocolate pudding fingerpaint, 22
  Dancing raisins, 59
  Fast stamp from foot padding, 9
  Fizz factor, 67
  Make your own peanut butter, 25
  Marshmallow project, 28
  Planetarium, 63
  Sandpaper pictures, 17
  Science shorts, 74-75
  Shaving cream body art, 3
  Shining your pennies, 65
  Straw and pipecleaner constructs, 7
  Tap shoes, 6
  Vegetable vehicles, 20

R

Radio show, 128
Robot costume, 40
Rubber
  bones, 64
  stamp, 38
Rubber band ball, 4

S

Sachets, 118
Salt dough, 14-15
Sand casting, 92-93
Sandpaper pictures, 17
Scarecrow, 94-95
Science projects, 53-75
Scrapbooks, 123
Screen pictures, 16
Seasonal scrapbook, 123
Seed cards, 115
Shaving cream body art, 3
Shining your pennies, 65
Shoes, tap, 6
Snowmen, white chocolate, 31
Soap
  crayon 2
  float, 3
Solar prints, 98
Spooky Halloween hands, 41
Spore
  prints, 96
  soup, 66
Sprouting
  beans, 54
  seeds, 115
Squirt Gun
  see Super squirt
Stained glass cookies, 30
Stamp
  from foot padding, 9

fruit flavored, 5
  rubber, 38
Standing ghost Halloween decoration, 39
Star dust, 74
Straw and pipecleaner constructs, 7
Styrofoam prints, 11
Sub in a cup, 75
Sugar
  crystals, 68-69
  cube art, 5
Superball, 4
Super squirt, 104-105

T

Tap shoes, 6
Thanksgiving decorations, 44
3-D salt map dough, 14-15
Time capsule, 122
Tin can lantern, 12-13
Tooth project, 70
Turkey, apple, 44

U

Underwater magnifier, 97

V

Vegetable vehicles, 20

W

Watch me grow, 74
Water
  dredge, 103
  experiment, 71
  play, 71; 104-105
Way water travels, 71
Weaving on driftwood, 78
Weird and wonderful pumpkins, 90-91
White chocolate snowmen, 31
Window decoration, 45